ALEXANDRA
DAVID-NÉEL

MARION DAPSANCE

ALEXANDRA DAVID-NÉEL

Spiritual Icon,
Feminist,
Anarchist

Copyright © 2021 Marion Dapsance
All rights reserved.

ISBN-13: 978-1-7331007-3-1

Library of Congress Catalog No: 2021935868

First edition

Cover illustration and formatting: Keith Carlson

JORVIK PRESS
5331 S Macadam Ave., Ste 258-424
Portland OR 97239
JorvikPress.com

About the Author

Marion Dapsance teaches courses in Anthropology, Methodology, Buddhism, and Intercultural Relations at the Catholic University in Paris. A researcher on Modern Buddhism, she is the author of several books and articles on contemporary Western Buddhism. She holds a PhD in Anthropology from the École Pratique des Hautes Études at the Sorbonne, Paris. An associate Professor at Unicervantès in Bogotá, Colombia, she has also taught the History of Buddhism in the West at Columbia University, New York.

Other books by Marion Dapsance:

Qu'ont-ils fait du bouddhisme?

Alexandra David-Néel, l'invention d'un myth

Les dévots du bouddhisme

Acknowledgements

The Robert H. N. Ho Family Foundation for their generous funding; the American Council of Learned Societies for the strong academic support they provided; Courtney Bender and the members of the Department of Religion at Columbia University, in particular Bernard Faure and Elizabeth A. Castelli; and Patricia Maillard and the Alexandra David-Néel Museum in Digne-les-Bains.

Contents

Introduction 1

1. Building the New Temple 9
   The Republicans' Fight against Religion   9
   The Socialist Connection and The Occult Tradition   16
   Initiation as the Modern Alternative to Revolution   21

2. The Great Initiate 29
   A Theosophist Called Mitra   29
   Sanskrit Vocalizations and Astral Projections   35

3. A Buddhist in *Fin-de-Siècle* Paris 49
   Did Alexandra David-Néel ever Claim to be a Buddhist?   49
   Discussing Buddhist Esotericism with Léon de Rosny   53
   Eclectic Buddhism and Official Buddhism   56
   The Buddha's Real Teachings   70

4. Daughter of the French Enlightenment 81
   The Victory of Materialism over Spiritualism   81
   Apostasy: a French Literary and Political Fashion   89
   Establishing The Reign of Rational Women   95

5. In the Buddha's Motherland 105
   The Orientalist Reporter   105
   The Psychical Landscapes of India   111

6. Entering History through the Gates of Lhasa 135

7. From Modern to Materialistic Buddhism 163

Chronology 167

Bibliography 169

References 177

Introduction

Alexandra David-Néel was one of the main contributors to the introduction of Buddhism in the West and perhaps the first to coin the term "Buddhist Modernism."[1] She has been celebrated as a Buddhist icon, a feminist, a great explorer, a prolific writer and, most prominently, the first European woman to enter Lhasa – on foot, in 1924.

Today, several French and Belgian streets, schools and public transport stations bear her name, as well as a literary award, a luxury tea, a Hermès scarf, and other fashionable goods. Many films, documentaries, stage plays, stories, cartoons and comics take her as their heroine. Her former house-turned-museum in the Alps receives thousands of visitors a year, mostly readers of her books from around the world and domestic tourists visiting the shrine of a local saint.

Marie-Madeleine Peyronnet, her last secretary and nurse, has devoted her life to celebrating her late employer's memory. She recalls how extraordinary the old lady was, how modestly she lived and how entirely dedicated to spirituality she was. It is true that her rooms are totally devoid of any comfort or coquetry; the bed, armchair and desk are cheap and Spartan. Witnessing these living conditions, the Dalai Lama testified, "Here indeed lived a great Buddhist."

When asked about the kind of Buddhist practices Alexandra David-Néel performed, Marie-Madeleine Peyronnet is positive that she never saw her practice any kind of meditation or ritual

– because, she explains, Buddhism is not a religion but a way of life, a "philosophy for the intellectuals."

In what sense, then, was David-Néel "a great Buddhist," revered by so many artists and intellectuals – including the American writers, Jack Kerouac, Allen Ginsberg, Gary Snyder and Alan Watts? Who was she, how did she contribute to the introduction of Buddhism in the West, and what was her specific conception of this Asian tradition?

There have been many works dedicated to Alexandra David-Néel since her death in 1969: complete biographies, literary portraits, travel books, essays, anthologies of texts, feminist case studies, and academic articles. However, they tend to be either an expression of profound and unquestioned admiration for their subject or, in the case of the scattered academic texts that can be found in many languages, technical answers to specific questions.[2]

Each of those biographical works is of specific interest, whether it is a detailed account of her travels, an attempt to understand her psychology through an inquiry into her childhood, or a depiction of the cultural context of her time. However, none of them tries to illuminate David-Néel's true motivations for her Eastern travels, nor the exact conception of her Buddhism.

David-Néel has mostly – if not entirely – been treated as a simple bridge or cultural interpreter between the West and the East. She is said to have discovered the true essence of Buddhism in Paris, then travelled to Asia, where she supposedly found the exact same Buddhism and whole-heartedly practiced it with Tibetan masters before being recognized as a real lama herself. Then, full of compassion for the materialist Western world and convinced that Tibetan Buddhism was the best remedy for its ailments, she reluctantly went back to Europe to disseminate the Buddha's teachings through her numerous books and conferences.

This tale may have all the advantages of simplicity, but nothing could be further from the truth.

David-Néel was a convinced believer in materialism and had always fought for the reign of science above all forms of religion, which she considered mere superstition. She therefore never thought that Tibetan Buddhism was going to save the West thanks to its "spirituality." She never believed in spirituality. For her, there was just matter. Everything else is an illusion.

The persistent and simplistic legend that depicts Alexandra David-Néel as a kind of spiritual bridge between East and West not only ignores the basic assumptions of her worldview but also considerably diminishes her role in the reception of Buddhism in the West. For she was not a simple convert, she was a creator. She invented a very specific form of modern Buddhism, largely based on the French anticlerical and positivist traditions of the 19th century. This trend of modern Buddhism is still alive on a global level and seems to cohabit quite peacefully with other very different and contradictory trends.

"Modern Buddhism" and "Buddhist Modernism" are the two phrases used by historians and social scientists today to identify certain trends that emerged, during the late 19th and 20th centuries, in the evolution of Buddhist doctrines and practices. According to the historian of religion David McMahan, Buddhist Modernism refers to a distinct recent phenomenon both in Asia and the West, characterized by a rejection of some aspects of tradition that constituted the flesh of Asian forms of Buddhism but seemed "irrational" or outdated to western converts and Buddhist reformists[3]. Certain texts, doctrines, precepts, myths and beliefs were considered unjustified in the name of science (whereas others on the contrary were deemed "scientific"), and many social, ritual and devotional practices were either reinterpreted in psychological terms or relinquished altogether in the name of democracy, reason and individualism.

Similar and anterior to McMahan's approach is Donald Lopez's notion of Modern Buddhism, defined as "an international Buddhism that transcends cultural and national boundaries, creating… a cosmopolitan network of intellectuals, writing most often in English." This new Buddhist school claims that ancient Buddhism fundamentally shared modern ideals of "reason, empiricism, science, universalism, individualism, tolerance, freedom and the rejection of religious orthodoxy."

These forms of Buddhism emerged at the end of the 19th century as a result of the crisis of the West's Christian faith on the one hand and the decolonization of Southeast Asia on the other.[4] This specific historical background had previously been explored by the German Indologist and Buddhologist Heinz Bechert,[5] who was the first scholar to use the phrase Buddhist Modernism to describe the late 19th-century religious and political polemics that gave birth to the definition of Buddhism as a rational philosophy.

Donald Lopez and David McMahan seem to understand the phenomenon in the same light, with Donald Lopez insisting on the internal unity of modern Buddhism as a school in its own right, with its own lineages, ideas and textual references, and David McMahan seeking to uncover the ideological and cultural forces, whether explicit or implicit, responsible for the emergence of various hybrid forms of contemporary Buddhism. Whereas Donald Lopez bases his analyses on historical data that highlights the importance of both theological arguments and political agendas in the emergence of a new definition of Buddhism, McMahan defends a more philosophical approach, with a focus on the "construction of modern identity," as defined by Charles Taylor in *Sources of the Self*[6] – a definition of modernity that might actually be more intellectual abstraction than historical fact.

As a complement to these approaches, I would like to propose another way to look at modern Buddhism: as a discourse on man in society that uses available knowledge on Buddhism to reformulate and give weight to certain progressive ideas of the time. These discourses focus on the necessity for individuals to liberate themselves from all possible obstructions and consequently to transform society for the better. It is a specific kind of discourse, which does not consist in the simple exposition, renovation or defense of an original Buddhist doctrine, but rather in the identification of the current state of evil in the developed world, in the revelation of its cause and in the proposition of a remedy.

This threefold articulation constitutes a soteriology, or discourse on salvation, as defined by the French anthropologist Wiktor Stoczkowski.[7] Such discourses usually give rise to various existential, social, and political projects, for the Buddhist remedy has to be applied in some way or other. Those movements may claim to be Buddhist or Buddhist-based, they are often only partly or superficially so, as Stephen Prothero has successfully shown in the case of the American Buddhist reformer, Henry Steel Olcott.[8] This definition of modern Buddhism as movements based on soteriological discourses about the West may be heuristically fruitful, as it offers both neutrality and a concern for historicity: it does not take for granted or define in advance what the terms "modern" or "traditional" actually refer to, but it tries to describe in detail what Buddhists really mean and refer to when they associate certain words and ideas with Buddhism (reason, individualism, spirituality, science, etc.). This should help us get a clearer sense of the worldviews the devotees aim to promote. Besides, this definition also redefines and restricts the distinction between traditional and modernist approaches to Buddhism.

I shall refrain from drawing the line between either East and West, pre- and post-20th century, or orthodoxy and innovation, since there has always been innovation, and the latest form taken by any cultural practice can always be deemed modern, whatever the period. Instead, I shall consider modern any kind of movement, self-identified as Buddhist, that features a discourse and a set of corresponding practices concerned with the salvation of the West (or the Western way of life), knowing that each movement and thinker has a distinct understanding of modernity, of Buddhism, and of the practical Buddhist remedy they should offer the world.

Henry Steel Olcott's definition of those terms was in some respect quite different from his Theosophist associate Helena Petrovna Blavatsky's, while her definition is not exactly that of today's modern Buddhists, who in turn have quite a different view from Alexandra David-Néel's. The internal unity and variety of the modern Buddhist sect, as mapped by Donald Lopez, may only be described after comparing the worldviews and practices of several movements and people identifying as modern Buddhists.

This book is both an intellectual biography and a contribution to the study of modern Buddhism. It intends to retrace Alexandra David-Néel's intellectual and spiritual evolution by identifying the places, networks, figures and doctrines that led her to formulate her own definition and practice of Buddhism. It reflects on the complex journey of a singular travel-writer, delving back into her Catholic youth (she was once tempted by the Carmelite order) and into her socialization in anarchist and socialist groups through her father and one of her closest friends, Jean Hautstont, both radical activists. That initial stage of her intellectual formation led her to lose her Christian faith and adopt a materialist and atheistic worldview that seems incompatible with her glorification as a spiritual master.

In parallel with her political activities, Alexandra David joined various esoteric societies, including the Theosophical Society, which aroused her interest in both occult phenomena and Asian philosophical traditions. Under the influence of the Theosophist, socialist and feminist Annie Besant, Alexandra David also became a Freemason in the first French feminist lodge, *Le Droit Humain* (The Human Right) and started a career as a freelance journalist for socialist and feminist newspapers.

She deepened her interest in Asian cultures in the recently opened Parisian Museum of Asian Arts. It is probably under the influence of its founder, Émile Guimet, a rich industrialist, traveler and connoisseur, that Alexandra David decided to start her ethnographical journeys East. In the context of the European discovery of the Buddha and his teachings, she developed an idiosyncratic understanding of Asian doctrines, including Buddhism, which she associated with anarchist and libertarian philosophies. While in her thirties she continued writing for feminist and socialist newspapers, advocating women's economic independence rather than their political rights.

In 1892, she had to start earning a living – her parents did not accept her becoming a Theosophist and stopped sending her money. With some professional training – a diploma in music from the Brussels Conservatory was her only qualification – she decided to launch a career as an opera singer. She performed in various theaters in Paris, in other parts of France and in the French colonies of Indochina and Tunisia.

Reversing her independent feminist stance, she agreed to marry her then-lover, a railway engineer established in Tunis, Philippe Néel. She was 36 years old and insisted she did not want to be a housewife and mother. It probably was a marriage of convenience – at least on her part. Indeed, only a few days after her wedding, she left her husband to travel across Europe and North Africa, and under the pretext of a lingering neurasthenia demanded that he finance her trip to India.

The journey should have lasted a few months, but she did not return to France until 14 years later, wreathed in glory. Actively promoting herself through the media of her time (she notably made extensive use of photography), she made herself known as a specialist in Tibet and its culture, producing at a blistering pace many repetitive books about her Himalayan adventures and the mysteries of Oriental traditions. She readily embraced the established and lucrative literary traditions – the adventure novel in Jules Verne fashion, the travel story in both Romantic and journalistic styles, the esoteric treatise revealing secret knowledge in Theosophical customs and, with much less enthusiasm, scholarly books complying with the standards of the emerging discipline of Tibetology.

At the end of her life – she died at the age of 101 – she witnessed the growing fascination of younger generations with Asian religions and the European importation of Tibetan religions by lamas. While she never practiced Tantric rituals or meditations outside of her ethnographic experiments in Asia, she was promoted as a Tibetan Buddhist icon by the first Western converts, who came to her Provençal house – renamed Samten Dzong, the Fortress of Meditation – to seek her spiritual guidance and advice. She was also given a new name, "Lamp of Wisdom," a translation of a Tibetan title she received from her main influence, an ascetic from Sikkim.

Alexandra David-Néel was a fascinating witness to and creator of modern Buddhism, not only for the adventurous life she led but also because she was at the forefront of the Western invention of a world religion named Buddhism. She was actively participating in a movement that involved scholars, Theosophists, curators, translators, travelers and ethnographers, missionaries and colonials, Hindu reformers, occultists, socialists, Himalayan kings, and Tibetan monks. But she was doing so from the awkward position of a middle-aged, self-educated, jobless, penniless and lonely French woman. And it is probably because of all the hardship she had to overcome to gain access to the various arenas where new forms of Buddhism were being invented that her ideas became so original – and often misunderstood.

Trying to understand her Buddhist Modernism is the objective of this book.

1

Building the New Temple

There shall be no more an appeal to arms, but to justice; no longer a crying after a God Who hides Himself, but to Man who has learned his own Divinity. The Supernatural is dead; rather, we know that it never yet has been alive. What remains is to work out this new lesson, to bring every action, word, and thought to the bar of Love and Justice; and that will be, no doubt, the task for years. Every code must be reversed; every barrier thrown down; party must unite with party, country with country, and continent with continent. There is no longer the fear of fear, the dread of the hereafter, or the paralysis of strife. Man has groaned long enough in the travails of birth; his blood has been poured out like water through his own foolishness; but at length he understands himself and is at peace.

Robert Hugh Benson, *Lord of the World*, 1907

The Republicans' Fight against Religion

Understanding the French and specifically the Parisian political context around the time of David-Néel's birth is crucial to understanding her intellectual formation. During the 19th century, Paris became a gigantic and parasitic outgrowth that threatened the whole country's health. Indeed, historians have shown that during the first half of the century, the French capital expanded in an uncontrolled and dangerous way.[9] Starting with 500,000 inhabitants in 1801, Paris had grown to more than 1 million in 1850, and 2 million in 1870. The city was too small to absorb such demographic pressure, and the sanitary conditions were insufficient to maintain an acceptable level of hygiene. The Parisian people became sick, especially in the parts of town populated by the working class, who kept coming from the countryside to get jobs in the city's factories and sweatshops, as described by Hugo and Zola.

The divide between the rich and poor was aggravated by Haussmann's works, which sought to remedy the situation with the construction of wide, clean avenues. That actually led to a sharp segregation; the well-off remained in central Paris, while the lower classes were relocated to the outskirts of town, which soon became known as the "the red belt." In fact, a revolutionary movement was emerging from the *faubourgs* (Montmartre, Belleville), which threatened the people living in the centre. There was fear on one side, hatred and resentment on the other. That popular movement would later be called the Commune, an allusion to the 1789 Revolution, and later theorized as communist by Marx.

The city was then already in a bad situation when the war with Prussia broke out on July 19, 1870. Led by Louis Napoléon in person, the army failed to resist the enemy and was trapped in Sedan on September 1. Taken prisoner, the Emperor capitulated. It was the end of the Second Empire. On September 4, Republican activists, followed by the *faubourgs* crowd, invaded the streets of the capital and stormed City Hall, where a temporary Republican government was proclaimed. Its primary objective was to protect the country from the Prussian invasion, hoping to organize elections when the war was over.

The population, burning with patriotic fever, took up arms. The ideals of 1792 were resuscitated: *levée en masse, salut public*, the organization of victory, even terror, if that was necessary, and "commune." The revolutionaries organized themselves. Each quarter of the city had its club where politics was discussed and where vigilance committees reaffirmed their dedication to the defence of the revolution against reactionary forces. These cadres united into one Central Committee, which proposed a political programme: all-out war, a Republican, democratic and socialist government, and an egalitarian distribution of food through rationing and requisitions.

The Central Committee was first conceived as an auxiliary to the official French government in its fight against Prussia but soon became a political opponent. Paris fell prey to civil war, with an agitated populace unwilling to disarm while confronting the government, which, according to the most violent factions, was not radical enough in its political reforms. It was clear the revolutionaries would not stop fighting and in fact were starting to build an autonomous political entity. The government duly decided to eradicate the movement.

On March 18, the army marched on Paris, arrested two Republican generals, and executed them in public. That only further inflamed the revolt. Fearing for its security, the government immediately relocated to Versailles. The Central Committee then seized control of City Hall, which was vacant, and declared the birth of the Commune, giving it the appearance of a counter-government, composed of several ministers: Finances, Justice, Education, Work, External Relations, General Safety – on the model of the 1793 institutions.

Historians are still not sure exactly what the Commune aimed to achieve. Impose its authority on the entire country? Wait until a truly Republican government was elected on a national scale? Become an autonomous entity, independent of the rest of the country?

To contemporaries, the situation was ambiguous and uncertain, too. Some Proudhonian socialists tried to provide a theoretical justification – the Commune was the first step towards the destruction of the nation. France would become a federal entity, composed of many independent towns. Marx also famously commented on the events, seeing in the Parisian rebellion the proof of his theories on the class struggle and the necessary dissolution of the State. However, these two theories conflicted with the traditional Jacobin party, for which the nation was "One and Indivisible."

The only common goal of the rebels was the proclamation of a new Republic and its defence against the official government in Versailles. Before the government finally supressed the insurrection in May 1871 – arresting over 40,000, of whom 13,000 were convicted – the Commune enacted several measures that prefigured the Third Republic: the separation of Church and State, the project of free, secularized, compulsory schooling. Although ideologically disparate, the Republicans, mostly workers, employees, craftsmen, teachers and house servants, shared the same philosophical vision for their country. They wanted to achieve the Enlightenment's ideal – eradicate Christianity's influence on society, culture and the popular mind.

In fact, the civil war of 1870-1871 between the Republicans and the Emperor's supporters was not just a conflict between two social groups with different visions of the state. It was also a war of religions, the opposition of two different faiths: Catholicism and rationalism.[10] The Republicans did not accept the control exercised by the Catholic Church in France, especially in education and burials. They wanted their children educated away from the Catholic faith and clergy. Expanding on their right since 1792 to get married without the approval of the Church, they now also wanted their dead buried by a civil servant rather than a priest.

The opponents of the Church followed the anticlerical and anti-Christian tradition founded by Voltaire and his fellow Encyclopaedists. They promoted Reason over prejudices, dogmas and superstitions and actively wrote and distributed pamphlets denouncing the abuses of the Church and making fun of religion's "stupidity." Since the 1848 revolution, these activists had organized themselves in associations on the model of the Revolution's philosophical clubs, often located in cafés and called Free Thought Societies.[11] These associations, largely composed of the working class and presided over by schoolteachers and sometimes eminent scientists, published newspapers and leaflets which they sold cheaply in the street. They also organized civil funerals, marriages and even baptisms. Indeed, the Free Thought movement had its own rituals, liturgies, sacred texts, priests and beliefs, which they tried to impose on the rest of society through preaching and law-making.

However, French society remained profoundly Christian, and the Republicans' hope of creating an alternative religion came to nothing. Nonetheless, their efforts did prefigure a change to the French Constitution in 1905 with the separation of Church and State, a political principle that prevails and is highly valued today.

It is to this politico-philosophical tradition that David-Néel's father belonged and into which he initiated his daughter. Louis David (1815-1904) was a schoolteacher and a Republican activist from the Loire region. He was the son of a soldier, Pierre David, and a dressmaker, Anne Colombe Ménétrié. The David family was originally Protestant, but Louis David was baptised a Catholic at the cathedral of Tours. His father Pierre was a Freemason in the Sons of the Loire lodge, a schoolteacher for some time and Deputy Mayor of his small town.

The son followed in his father's footsteps – Louis David also became a schoolteacher, a Freemason and a political activist. But his superiors and the local bourgeoisie took a dim view of his pursuits, and he was dismissed from his teaching position. He moved to another small town and became the school headmaster but was again berated for lack of professionalism. It seems he was more interested in politics than education.

As a keen Republican activist, Louis David participated in the first "Republican banquets" that took place in Paris on July 9, 1847, a few months before the revolution broke out. Apparently an atheist, he objected to the tradition of beginning the banquets with a prayer. In February 1848 he was in Paris for an extended period to take part in the revolution. In June 1848 he was once more criticised by his superiors for abandoning his school responsibilities, for "disseminating the most subversive socialist propositions" and for being a "provocative agent of disorder and anarchy: [he] declaimed against property, excited workers to demand a reduction in working hours, an increase in wages, foreshadowing an organized strike."

In August 1848, he was dismissed from his post by the Minister of Instruction for leaving his school and going to Paris without permission. The Minister mentioned in his letter to the rector of the Indre-et-Loire district that Louis David had also created a Club that was "apparently dissolved" but was actually still active as a "secret society." The Minister advised keeping him under strict surveillance, for "he [was] professing opinions and carrying out activities that [were] extremely dangerous for the tranquillity of the country."

In 1849 Louis David stood for election as a Member of Parliament. He resigned from his job and became a journalist for socialist newspapers. In 1851 he published a book on how to "make work instruments available to workers in all occupations." On December 2, 1851 protesters demonstrated in Tours against Louis Napoléon Bonaparte's coup. Louis David was among a dozen violent protesters arrested and sent to prison. On December 31 Louis David's mother, Anne Colombe David, sent a letter to Louis Napoléon Bonaparte begging for mercy for her son, reminding him of her late husband's faithful military career. Louis David remained in prison until he was tried in March 1852 and expelled from France. He took refuge in Belgium with other political activists.

In 1854, still in Belgium, Louis David, aged 39, met and married Alexandrine Borghmans, aged 22, who came from a bourgeois Catholic family. After the 1859 political amnesty, the couple relocated to Paris.[12] Louise Alexandrine Marie was born on October 24, 1868 in the bourgeois Parisian suburb of Saint-Mandé. The family then moved to east Paris to a home on the Cours de Vincennes.

When the 1871 revolution broke out and was crushed, Louis David took his three-year-old daughter to the "Mur des fédérés" to show her the activists' cadavers being hurriedly tossed into mass graves. This undoubtedly left a deep impression on her. She would always remember her father's words: "Men are cruel to each other."[13] In an unpublished letter to her husband, Alexandra David-Néel mentioned that her father remained a freethinker, atheist, and freemason until his death in 1904.[14]

There were, in fact, two main tendencies in French Free Thought during the 19th century. Some free-thinkers were deist – they still believed in a God, though not in a traditional Christian way, their abstract God sometimes being associated with a higher scientific principle. Then there was the spiritualist trend, whose adherents believed in a spiritual realm independent of the material world depicted by biologists and physicians, and not necessarily related to a God. On the fringes, other free-thinkers were atheist and materialist, rejecting the idea of anything existing beyond the material realm, be it a God or a soul, since only science could answer man's questions about life.

The first lineage of thought can be traced back to Rousseau and Robespierre, who still believed in a Great Clockmaker and in the survival of the soul after death. The second lineage was established in the 18th century by philosophers such as Voltaire, Diderot, La Mettrie, Helvetius, d'Holbach and Condillac, who claimed there is nothing in the world but matter in constant evolution, perceptible through the sensations, with man perceived as a wild beast,[15] and the illusion of a spirit or soul resulting from a mishmash of information channelled through the senses. Materialism became the dominant ideology in French Free Thought during the second half of the 19th century, with the works of Darwin and other scientists understood as its definitive confirmation.

The Socialist Connection and The Occult Tradition

Catholic conceptions of the human being and society had long been brought into question. These values had been denounced as a source of injustice by the Enlightenment philosophers, and their social and political foundations had been destroyed by the French Revolution and partially replaced by nebulous Republican worldviews. This led many French citizens in the 19th century to seek a different source of revelation (other than God and the Church) to shape a new worldview and build the perfect society. The belief blossomed that the most accurate – and therefore supposedly the truest and fairest – source of moral, social and political norms had to be science.

Science thus provided a new set of criteria for determining not only the real but also the ideal. Science could tell us what the world was like and, most importantly, how it should be. Some thinkers like Comte, Saint-Simon, Prosper Enfantin, and Fourier considered science to be a religion in its own right, fully equipped to provide a new, fairer basis for the establishment of a harmonious society. Others, in contrast, believed science was not enough without recourse to the indispensable aspects of tradition.

The emergence of what are usually labelled occultism and esotericism is best understood in the context of this visionary "scientific" reconstruction of Western civilization. As the historian of religions Julian Strube has convincingly shown,[16] those terms (and the traditions they refer to) are products of the 19th century rather than a mere continuation or revival of centuries-long traditions of "rejected knowledge."[17]

The French socialist tradition that developed spiritualist theories under the July Monarchy became marginalized after the materialist Marxist trends of socialism triumphed in 1848. They were forced to develop their theories about humanity and the ideal society with discretion – hence the term occult. It is only later, in the late 1880s, that the myriad groups and individuals interested in magic, Kabbalah, astrology, Tarot, mysticism, Orientalism, Gnosticism and the like started to define themselves as unified, coherent esoteric or occult traditions influenced by pre-1848 socialism.

The synthesis that took the name occultism was inspired by the establishment of the Theosophical Society in France and was essentially based on the work of Alphonse-Louis Constant (1810-1875). Also known as Éliphas Lévi, Constant was a former Seminarist who became a radical socialist under the July Monarchy and later made a name for himself as a master of magic and Kabbalah. At the beginning of his career he claimed, like many others, that socialism was true Christianity and that men should work together to establish God's kingdom on earth. He became interested in Saint-Simonianism and Fourierism, the two main utopias of the day, but was soon disappointed after concluding they were overly preoccupied with economy and industry, or too eccentric.[18]

He then took an active part in the 1848 revolution, at the head of a political association called *Club de la montagne* (an allusion to Robespierre). He later published many books on social and religious topics, both under his real name and pen names. His 1859 *Histoire de la magie* consecrated him as a renowned magician, and he started initiating disciples. At the end of his life, he became a Freemason but resigned a few years later because the Pope excommunicated all secret societies and because the Freemasons became increasingly materialist.[19] Ultimately, Lévi had always wanted, both as a socialist and as a Kabbalist and magician, to determine what true Christianity was and then to implement it.

Éliphas Lévi was forgotten for a decade and re-emerged as the source of a specifically French occult tradition that the new generation aimed to restore. Their goal was to oppose materialism and, just as importantly, what they considered the false doctrine taught by the Theosophical Society. Undeniably, in the mid-1870s, the latter was gaining considerable momentum with its novel, original ideas and was posing a serious threat to French spiritualists. Notably, Madame Blavatsky's notion that "true mysticism" was to be found in the East rather than in the West was unbearable to them, as they still drew their inspiration from Biblical commentaries by various European thinkers.

Gérard Encausse (1865-1916), also known as Papus, was a physician who developed an interest in Alchemy, Spiritism and Mesmerism and looked unfavourably on both the materialistic trends developing in Freemasonry and the "Oriental" ideas defended by the founders of the Theosophical Society. In order to protect "true, Western mysticism," he founded a new journal in 1888 called *L'Initiation* and in 1891 a new initiatory order, which he named the Martinist Order – after Louis-Claude de Saint-Martin, an 18th-century Illuminist. Papus, who had been initiated into many different secret societies, including the

Kabbalist Order of the Rose-Cross, the French Gnostic Church, the Hermetic Order of the Golden Dawn, and Swedenborgian Freemasonry, said he received an initiation by one of Saint-Martin's disciples. The co-founder of the Martinist Order was another self-declared initiate of Saint-Simon, Augustin Chaboseau, a historian and journalist who worked for *La Fronde*, the feminist newspaper that Louise David also wrote for, and who was a friend of Maria Deraismes, the famous feminist activist who would create the first female Freemason lodge (into which Louise David was initiated) and later become a librarian and curator at the Musée Guimet.[20]

The Martinist Order thus became "a counter-model to Theosophy à la française."[21] It can best be described as a Gnostic-Christian type of Freemasonry, with its complex system of hierarchy, secrecy and initiatory ceremonies centred on Biblical heterodox commentaries.[22] Other pre-existing doctrines and practices, such as Kabbalah, Tarot, Mesmerism, "Egyptian knowledge," etc. that were not yet called occult or esoteric in any specific way were often grafted on Papus' reinvented French tradition, or at least reinterpreted according to his definition.

Madame Blavatsky herself, who had accidentally triggered the creation of an "ancient tradition of occultism" in France, defined occultism in *Isis Unveiled* (1877) in terms of the works of Éliphas Lévi and Papus. Since they had common references and sources of inspiration, Papus and Blavatsky developed similar theories about the human and the divine: a naturalistic and supernatural understanding of man (i.e., a conception that blends both materialistic science and ancient Biblical commentaries on the notion of the soul), a Gnostic understanding of the creation, and a pantheistic conception of God. Their main difference, however, resided in Papus' notion that true mysticism was to be found in the West (i.e., in Christianity and Judaism) rather than the East (i.e., in Indian religions). Unlike Madame

Blavatsky, Papus was also interested in politics and published political tracts on his progressive outlook on mankind.[23]

It is in the context of this rivalry between two modern schools of esotericism – the French school, mostly based on Biblical commentaries, and the Anglo-Saxon Theosophical movement, which increasingly relied on Indian materials discovered by British colonial officers – that Louise David's trajectory in the esoteric scene should be understood. From her private notebooks and posthumously published memories, it seems she was first interested in Gnostic approaches to the Bible before discovering the new "oriental" interpretation applied to the notion of occult tradition by the Theosophical Society.

Indeed, in *Le Sortilège du mystère*[24] she writes that she started to question her Catholic faith on discovering that other interpretations of the Bible and of Jesus' identity were possible. This happened when she was 12 – long before being taught from Renan's *Vie de Jésus* (1863) in anarchist and socialist circles. Then, in Catholic boarding school, she discussed theological issues, notably the Trinity, with two or three foreign Protestant girls studying there who were exempted from going to mass, much to the surprise of the young Louise.

One of those girls, as we shall see, later wrote to her from London, sending a brochure expounding the teachings of an English Gnostic society. In *Lampe de sagesse*[25] she also wrote praises to "the Eternal" for having "saved her from idolatry" (i.e., Catholicism) and for having made her "understand and admire the sublime harmony of heaven." These words sound like a Gnostic profession of faith. She was then in her twenties. The same year (1889), she wrote that Jesus was her "master" (rather than savior), along with Epictetus and the Stoics[26] and that she had "the ambition to join and resuscitate for (herself) a philosophy illustrated by so many great men."[27] This is a clear allusion to the secret tradition of either the French occultists or the Anglo-Saxon Theosophists.

Initiation as the Modern Alternative to Revolution

In France, the year 1889 holds special importance for anyone interested in exotic religious views. That year, the French musicologist, philosopher and poet Édouard Schuré published *Les Grands Initiés*,[28] which became an instant and lasting bestseller. Schuré (1841-1929) was a French artist who denounced the hegemony of materialistic science over the culture of the time. He feared new generations were condemned to live in spiritual drought, unable to turn to the Church for succor, as their fathers once did. He thought the Church had departed from Christ's original teachings and could only spout rigid dogmas in its stand against science. Although it still had a rich repertoire of symbols and ceremonies, the Church had lost track of their profound meanings and thus rendered them sterile and useless.

Science, on the other hand, had focused on matter to the detriment of the spirit and led many contemporaries to despair.[29] If there was no other reality than the physical/biological aspect of life, if human life was just the result of an instinct to survive in a competitive environment where the strongest destroy the weak, if there was no other motivation than the satisfaction of needs and the gratification of pleasure, then it meant that humanity was nothing more than a species of intelligent animal, with no possibility of improving over time.

That view, which Louise David finally adopted, was anathema to Schuré and his readership. There had to be a middle way between the nihilistic philosophies that emerged in the late 19th century and the outdated institutionalized religions. It is this middle way that Schuré described in *Les Grands Initiés*.

Though original in form, the book is little more than an exposition, in clear and elegant language, of the complex theories developed by Madame Blavatsky in *Isis Unveiled* (1877) and *The Secret Doctrine* (1888). Schuré had either read these books or learned about them in the *Revue spirite*, a journal devoted to the dissemination of Theosophical ideas in France.[30]

In his colourful epic, Schuré, acting as a new Dante, guides the reader through the different stages of human history, from the most superficial aspects of religions to the very heart of their eternal truth. The reader starts with the story of the Aryan great ancestor Rama, who established the worship of the sacred fire, explained the world in astrological terms and reformed his society, and finishes with Jesus, "the master of the masters" who revealed the true nature of God and the real Gnostic meaning of resurrection. Along the way, the reader learns the progressive revelations brought by Krishna, Hermes, Moses, Orpheus and Pythagoras and is instructed in their "mysteries." Each chapter brings the reader closer to the holy of holies represented by Jesus' true revelation, with support from contemporary, but often controversial, historical knowledge. The book is thus conceived as an initiation in itself. To follow the author's metaphor, the reader, like humanity in the course of its history, is led from the outside of the temple to its inner sanctuary.

The metaphor of the temple or the cathedral resonates among the French occultists of the time (and of today). It allows them to explain the different aspects of religions – and religious plurality itself – by distinguishing between their outer, "exoteric" meaning and their inner, eternal, and universal "esoteric" one. It is quite likely that Louise David was familiar with this metaphor and influenced by it in her later approach to exotic religions.

For most people, so explain the occultists, a cathedral is the building wherein a religious institution, the Church, publicly delivers its official teachings and rituals. A cathedral contains certain objects, images, numbers, or gestures that have an obvious meaning and function for the Christian people, a meaning relayed through a social environment deeply steeped in Christian culture. The labyrinth, for example, may seem mysterious to us today, but its symbolism was clear to people of the time, as was its function. It represented the ascension of Christ, and penitents had to trace its complicated path on their knees to follow him to heaven.

Other symbols found in cathedrals that appeared purely decorative to most people had precise meaning for some individuals, who claimed to have secretly learned them orally from older initiates. The term "initiates" in a modern European context originally indicated the Freemasons – architects and workers instructed in all the secrets of cathedral building. The term came to be applied later to their numerous avatars, the Rosicrucians, the Martinists, the Theosophists, etc. The Freemasons originally were local fraternities of stonemasons who taught novices the secrets of their craft, which may have included symbolic aspects of architecture, mathematics, physical orientation, etc. When the art of building cathedrals disappeared, or so it is said, Freemasonry survived as "speculative Freemasonry," secret fraternities engaged in religious symbolism and devoted to the art of building society – in other words, politics.[31] Most secret and initiatory societies in the West are based on the Freemason model, both in structure and worldview.

The initiatory societies that flourished in the 19th century remained faithful to the conviction that images, objects and words sometimes have special meanings that are not reducible to what the Church officially teaches. They also retained the idea that symbolic knowledge should be transmitted to selected individuals orally through ceremonial rites of passage.[32] With this approach, members of these societies interpreted symbols and articulated them in rituals that enabled each individual to get a personal, experiential understanding of the "universal doctrine" in which they believed – without knowing exactly what it was. Of course, in these circles the Truth is never revealed, as is the case in most religions. It is a subjective experience, an understanding of the world one needs to conceptualize for oneself in a way that still respects the symbolic language and basic assumptions these groups are built on.

The initiates' goal, however, is not only spiritual and individual: it is also political. The initiates seek to "rebuild the temple" (i.e., society) from the inside out, based on the knowledge hidden "within the cathedral" (i.e., in the symbolic interpretation of all religious traditions). They wish to establish a new earthly kingdom based on new notions of humanity, and this should be done through the creation and training of a new intellectual elite.[33]

One could say that Freemasonry and its 19th-century by-products, with their complex rituals and ceremonies, their dense doctrinal elaborations on symbols and legends perceived to be universal, and their aim of guiding humanity to a more harmonious future, are religions in all but name, halfway between a Church and a secular progressive ideology. They could even be called reformist or regenerative religions, since their main concern is the regeneration (rather than the salvation) of mankind.[34] The only ways they differ from other religions is by keeping their rituals closed to the public and not officially proclaiming their dogmas. The meaning behind the legends and symbols they discuss at "workshops" is always up for debate – within certain limits, of course. These groups do proclaim certain unquestionable truths and goals, which is especially true for the two predominant esoteric societies of the 19th century – Freemasonry and the Theosophical Society (Louise David was a long-time Theosophist):

- The search for the original and pure religion, wisdom, or science of humanity that would be compatible with the natural sciences and applicable to every culture.
- The goal of establishing a Universal Fraternity, based on a minimalist and consensual faith, to bring everlasting peace and justice to the world.
- The rejection of specific truths defined by Christianity and Judaism that are considered rigid dogmas (in fact, these groups reject most, if not all, Christian beliefs – a divine creator and personal God, an incarnate saviour, resurrection, original sin, heaven and hell, miracles, and so on).
- An evident disdain for official churches, echoed in the group's self-profiling as a higher-level, persecuted minority.
- The idea that Truth can be discovered only through rational discussion among initiates and is ultimately found within oneself.
- A belief in human progress, first in the individual, moral and intellectual realms and consequently on a global societal level (initiation is conceived as a milder and more effective alternative to revolution).
- The idea that progress is achieved through the efforts of a new spiritual elite, the initiates or great masters, who generally remain extremely discreet.

In a nutshell, these religions do not reject dogmas or rituals, though they do reject transcendence. According to advocates, no anthropology, philosophy, sociology, cosmology, or public policy should be based on any kind of recognized, publicly shared traditions – whether they be divine revelations or ancestral customs, which should all be purged as irrational. Human culture should be built anew on immanent, scientific, or rational grounds – that is to say, in accordance with the latest beliefs of a progressive intellectual elite. It is that specific brand of spirituality that interested Louise David at the end of the 19th century and which, in many ways, still characterizes modern Buddhism today.

Another implication of the cathedral metaphor involves an understanding of other religions – and that is crucial to understanding David-Néel's writings on Tibetan Buddhism. Like any religious buildings, objects, texts or images anywhere on the planet, the cathedral is a depository of symbols that cannot be fully explained by the cultural contexts in which they emerged. For this reason, though they claim to ground their knowledge in historical and anthropological facts, the occultists radically oppose the scientific method. Based on these premises (the belief in a single universal, ancestral doctrine at the heart of each civilization), occultists in the 19th century started comparing artefacts discovered in Egypt, India and Asia with their own European symbols and elaborated theories to make sense of such diversity.[35]

The universal use of shapes like the circle or the square, certain numbers like 3, and ideas like the mother-goddess or the judgment guaranteed to each person after death, led them to conclude that there existed a universal primitive religion hidden in every world religion, and that symbolism was its special language. To know the ultimate truth about life, the origin and end of humanity, and to understand why the world's cultures look so different, one had to be initiated.

Initiation in the 19th century could take many different forms, to which an unfulfilled Louise David would later add an even more radical option: spiritual travel to the Orient,[36] where she would look for living initiates, and thus continue to add to Schuré's list. Jesus was certainly not the last or the most perfect

– a belief she shared with Madame Blavatsky, Annie Besant and other Theosophists outside France. The progressive revelation of the secret doctrine by superior beings was not yet complete. It was necessary to look for new sources, and the Orient, now open to Westerners through colonial infrastructure, offered new opportunities for occultists. For the secret doctrine was not only a tradition received from past generations but was also an active collaboration by initiates to build a better future.

Before we delve into Louise David's personal initiations (which esoteric societies she entered as a novice, what she learned there, and how it changed the way she identified herself in the larger society), it is worth mentioning a third interpretation the occultists apply to the cathedral metaphor.

As we have seen, a cathedral or temple can be seen as a physical building belonging to the official Church, which delivers its superficial (and often erroneous) teachings. It can also be seen as a depositary of the universal truth, a museum of symbols to be decoded by a trained spiritual elite, a microcosm of the whole universe. The first option is called exoteric and is equivalent to a shell. The second is called esoteric and refers to the only valuable thing that resides in the shell, the pearl. One needs to open the first (which can quickly be discarded) to discover the second. That is done through the learning of symbols.

A third way to look at the cathedral is more physical and closer to the modern notion of science, in the most materialistic sense of the term. The cathedral, say the occultists, can be seen as the materialisation of ancient people's knowledge about the earth's magnetism. They claim all important monuments, especially religious ones, were built on the exact spots where the magnetic field is particularly strong. Or they were built near a water spring.

The same can be said about a cathedral's glass windows, which are interesting not primarily because they tell a story (exoteric dimension), or deliver secret symbols (esoteric one), but because, on a very physical level, they filter daylight in distinct ways and send specific visual stimuli to a person inside the building. The same is said about Gregorian and other sacred chants like Hindu and Buddhist mantras. The important thing is not what they explicitly or implicitly say, but the physical effect they have on people. We shall later see that this was the interpretative option David-Néel would finally choose, in accordance with the materialistic worldview she would eventually develop.

2

The Great Initiate

This time of intellectual regeneration and social transformation will come, we are sure. Already certain omens announce it. When Science knows, Religion can, and Man will act with new energy.

Édouard Schuré, *Les Grands Initiés*, 1889

A Theosophist Called Mitra

The young Louise David was looking for an elitist kind of spirituality that would set her apart from the French society of her time – and especially from contemporary French women, still predominantly Catholic. She must have longed to be initiated, as the tone of her notebooks suggests. Indeed, her notes clearly show that she firmly believed in her intellectual superiority and took great pride in the criticism she apparently endured from family and friends. She considered herself persecuted for her unorthodox ideas and constantly reassured herself that she was on the good path. Being rejected by "the idolaters" certainly was a sign of spiritual elevation.

Louise David seems to have discovered occultism in the late 1880s, not in France or Belgium but in England. She was then about 20. One of her girlfriends, probably from the Belgian Catholic convent where she was educated, was in England when she mailed her a "light blue brochure with bizarre drawings."[37] In her letter, the friend wrote that, since Alexandra had always been interested in religious matters, she should take a look at the writings issuing from "the Supreme Gnosis," which the friend identified as "an oriental sect." David-Néel explained that she had always been interested in religious topics, and serious theological discussions with classmates had truly disturbed her.[38] So she became very interested in the Supreme Gnosis. She recalls how impressed she was by "the enigmatic symbolism of the illustrated cover" of the booklet, "the particular jargon" used by the authors, "enamelled with words borrowed from the Sanskrit and from other exotic idioms that I did not know," the "odd doctrines" the authors were presenting "with an ultra-dogmatic assurance."[39] While she retrospectively describes herself as motivated by a purely intellectual and rather amused curiosity ("those people are mad!"), the young Louise was probably very interested in the spiritual truth the Supreme Gnosis offered, so much so that she decided to cross the English Channel to find out for herself.

It seems that the girlfriend in England connected Louise David with a certain Mrs. Morgan, who belonged to the Supreme Gnosis Society and other esoteric groups, including the Theosophical Society. The latter was founded in London in 1878, three years after its creation in New York by the Russian exile Helena Petrovna Blavatsky and the American journalist and lawyer Colonel Henry Steel Olcott. Mrs. Morgan, about whom no other information is given, kept sending her brochures from various secret societies, so Louise David became acquainted with a whole range of "similar little churches."[40]

After several weeks she went to London and met with Mrs. Morgan, who introduced her to the Supreme Gnosis Society. We do not know whether Louise David broke up with her family or left on cordial terms, though the first hypothesis seems most probable – especially with a 19th-century fervent Catholic mother. A family dispute would also explain why she did not have much money to support herself abroad and needed inexpensive accommodations in London, which she conveniently found through esoteric societies.

In *Le Sortilège* she describes in colourful prose her arrival at Victoria Station, her reception by the talented and psychologically disturbed young man who accompanied her to the Society, her meeting with a mysterious Mrs. Grant, vice-President of the Supreme Gnosis, "wearing pins and medals that may well have been insignia," and the down-to-earth experience she had in the bedroom allocated to her. On discovering in the morning light that the disquieting black windows she carefully inspected the night before, she found they hid nothing more supernatural than a mere garden. She also describes the daily activities of the society, mostly reading books in the library shrouded in Egyptian tobacco smoke, always on the lookout for invisible ghosts one must be careful not to sit on.[41]

David-Néel never tells her readers how she was initiated, explaining that the Supreme Gnosis repudiates the idea, which she also derides. However, she must have had some sense of being initiated at the time, even if her endorsement by the Supreme Gnosis did not involve any formal ceremony or ritual. Indeed, one can reconstruct her initiation if that term is understood as the progressive accession into a secret or semi-secret society with its specific rules, beliefs, hierarchies and customs, rather than a spectacular *mise-en-scène* that she first seemed to expect (and would later find in Freemasonry).

First, she writes[42] that one needed to have a "godmother" to enter the Society, as in Freemasonry. Mrs. Morgan acted as such, to assure the Society that the new constituent she was introducing was morally adequate. Then she explains that to be accepted by other members, the applicant needs to subscribe to its goals, namely "to form a confraternity of persons engaging themselves in the study of different religions and philosophies, especially those of the Orient" – a goal typical of 19th-century Anglo-Saxon esoteric societies. It is probably here at the Supreme Gnosis that she first became interested in Hindu and Buddhist traditions.

Finally, after being accepted by the other members, probably through correspondence (she must have written a cover letter explaining her motivations and good will, and sent it with Mrs. Morgan's reference testifying to her protégée's morality), and having been officially and quite ceremoniously escorted by the eccentric young man and welcomed to the house by the "mysterious" lady wearing unusual dress and jewels (in itself an initiation), Louise David had to comply with certain rules, practices and supernatural beliefs. This was all very different from what she was used to in the broader society – a specific sharing of space and allocation of time, the fact that invisible spirits or masters should be taken into account, the effort to appear indifferent to food and other worldly matters, and so on.

She also discovered that the Society was hierarchically organized, with a few people ostensibly endowed with supernatural powers at the top. Notably, she met a young French painter, Jacques Villemain, introduced to her as a "probationer," a candidate seeking the revelation of the higher teachings of the Society. He lived apart from other members, hidden in one of the best rooms, fasting most of the time, and he produced "dangerous" paintings which, according to the theory of the astral plane, observers could enter and then get lost forever.[43] People at the top of the spiritual hierarchy could deliver teachings to the less advanced, but this was quite exceptional, since a rule prevailed that "one should not speak of one's own realizations" – a rule that still exists in esoteric and Buddhist circles.

Both being French, Louise David and Jacques Villemain became close, and he acted as her main resource for details of the group's doctrine. It is probably through him and from books she borrowed from the Society's library that she gained her first knowledge of the secret doctrine, which she soon discovered was disputed by the numerous esoteric groups that existed in Europe.

She recalls that Villemain recounted her a tale of a man who "returned from death" – what today would be called a near-death-experience. The man was on a train with his wife and child going on vacation to the coast, when he suddenly realized the train had stopped and he was surrounded by silence and white fog. The wife and the little boy had left the train and were walking off. He followed, but only to a certain point, indicated by a thorny hedge, where a voice told him that he was "not expected." Then he sank into darkness and woke up in a hospital, a nurse at his bedside. His wife and son had been killed in a train accident; he had only been injured.[44] Writing several decades later, David-Néel commented that she had not understood (or believed) the story before hearing Tibetans expound on their doctrines on the after-death state. It is interesting to note that a century ago some Europeans were already comparing near-death experiences with Tibetan concepts of the afterlife – and already suspected that the Tibetans had the last word on the issue.

The young Alexandra did not stay long in London, not even a year. It was enough for her to improve her English, get a rudimentary grasp of Chinese and Indian literature from the Supreme Gnosis library and probably the British Museum, and to develop a distinct taste for "bizarre worlds populated by the most extravagant human specimens that can possibly be conceived" – a category in which she would later classify the Tibetans. Coming from an "eminently reasonable family" who lived "in a formalist atmosphere," she found such people and their beliefs entertaining and fresh: "When I say that I found those 'extravagant people' sympathetic, I do not mean I ever took them as role models. I simply watched them live their fantasies, being so naïve, so conceited, sometimes so brave, fighting against the secret and mysterious terrors their strange beliefs engendered. I also found them touching and pitiful, those tender hearts evolving in the dark, looking for sympathy and loving protection. What were the motives for their singular conduct? That is what I intended to discover."[45]

As already noted, it is unlikely that a romantic girl in her twenties, who had just written praises to God and issued other fervent religious declarations, had made a trip abroad simply to discover why other humans indulged in eccentric behaviors. While she certainly had become a kind of ethnologist by her fifties, when she embarked on her great Asian trip, her motivations in the late 1880s were probably more existential than scientific. Like many Europeans of the time, she wanted to find a spiritual alternative between the Church and the materialists' despair. She sought to be initiated, introduced into another kind of culture – and indeed she was. The esoteric knowledge she gained from the Supreme Gnosis proved useful much later when she decided to popularize Tibetan cultural practices in the West, for she had already absorbed the language, symbols and metaphors that that equipped her to understand exotic religions.

After her trip to London she returned to the continent. Deciding not to stay at her parents' home in Brussels, however, she established herself in Paris. It turned out that her parents did not approve of her new spiritual choices and declared she could not live at home while she frequented the Theosophical Society. She therefore had to earn her own living and find a place to stay.

Having studied piano during childhood and with a degree from the Brussels Conservatory, Louise David decided to launch a career as an opera singer. Paris in 1895 was the world capital of the arts, fashion and entertainment. She also followed Mrs. Morgan's advice and contacted the Parisian Lodge of the Theosophical Society, where she could find inexpensive accommodation and learn more about the secret doctrine. The Supreme Gnosis, she was told, was only a small school with limited resources and, if she wanted to progress in her Oriental studies, she needed to join the Theosophical Society. The organization would also provide a social network that would greatly facilitate her journeys East.

Her new life as an independent grown-up in Paris was therefore a step forward on both professional and spiritual levels. There she chose new names for herself, as proof she had become a new, initiated person: she became Alexandra David, Mitra, Alexandra Myrial and, years later after she got married, Alexandra David-Néel.

Sanskrit Vocalizations and Astral Projections

The Theosophical Society was founded in New York in 1875 by the Russian medium and expatriate, Helena Petrovna Blavatsky, and the American attorney, former journalist, and civil war veteran, Henry Steel Olcott, to elucidate cases of supernatural activity – communication with spirits, rapping, telepathy, automatic writing, ghostly apparitions, etc.

Later, the Society's goals included the formation of a "nucleus of the universal brotherhood of humanity" and the study of comparative religions. Madame Blavatsky was the Society's prophet and Olcott the association's president, in charge of all practical matters. In 1877 Madame Blavatsky published her first bestseller *Isis Unveiled* (four volumes), in which she expressed her initial ideas on supernatural phenomena, the cosmos and links between religions. She postulated the existence of an ancient religion common to all humanity.

In 1878 Blavatsky and Olcott moved to India, first to Mumbai (1878), then to Adyar (1882), to cooperate with the Arya Samaj, a Hindu reform movement founded by Swami Dayananda Saraswathi, in which they recognized values they shared.

It seems that, despite the success of *Isis Unveiled*, the Society was dormant. The move to India and their association with Hindu reformers was an attempt to gain new momentum – and the strategy proved successful. Indeed, this geographical location (closer to the source of Wisdom, away from Western materialism) and the relationships they established with Hindu and Buddhist reformers, Sinhalese nationalists, English colonials and journalists, and American Theosophists traveling in India, completely transformed the Society's scope and authority. Once an American spiritualist society among many others, whose apparent destiny was to sink into complete oblivion – as the Supreme Gnosis did – the Theosophical Society became one of the most culturally and politically influential groups of the late 19th century.

In 1879 Blavatsky and Olcott started a monthly magazine, *The Theosophist*, which soon gained wide readership, and introduced the idea of the "Mahatmas," the "great masters" of the "Fraternity" they wished to build in the world. Those mysterious, superior masters were said to be Indian men endowed with supernatural powers, whose compassion and wisdom enabled them to guide humanity on its path to spiritual perfection. They were to be found in hidden places in Tibet, the pristine roof of the world where the true religious doctrine could be preserved from decay.

Madame Blavatsky said she communicated with them through telepathy, automatic writing, or the materialisation of letters, which mysteriously fell from the ceiling or appeared in the cupboard. This innovative transformation of the traditional freemason great masters (those few anonymous people on top of the pyramid thought to control the world's destiny, for better or worse) into mysterious and beautiful Indians contributed greatly to the Society's success. These masters introduced a new type of mythology and later developed into an original, hybrid reformulation of Christian messianism, with the discovery of a new Indian "world saviour," Jiddu Krishnamurti, by Blavatsky's successor, the British socialist and feminist, Annie Besant.

We do not know whether Alexandra David approved of the quest for an Indian Christ but, though she later denied it, she was unquestionably influenced by the Theosophical Society in her own search for Oriental masters. In 1882 the Society established its headquarters in Adyar, where David-Néel would stay during her travels. From this base the Theosophical Society launched branches and sections[46] around the globe: North and South America, Australia, Asia and Europe.

It is worth noting that on a trip to Ceylon, Blavatsky and Olcott publicly converted to Buddhism, to the amazement of the Sinhalese elite. Their new English friend and collaborator, a journalist named Alfred Percy Sinnett, was appointed specialist in Esoteric Buddhism – that is, the reimagining of Buddhism in Theosophical terms with the help of Blavatsky's two prominent personae, mahatmas Koot Hoomi and Morya.[47] Although the Theosophists played a leading role in the revival of Buddhism in Ceylon and India (mostly through the work of Olcott, who wished to "reunify the Buddhist world" with the establishment of a canon, catechism and capital),[48] the Society shifted its interest from Buddhism to Hinduism.

In 1882, Madame Blavatsky became ill and decided to return to Europe. Olcott had convinced her to accompany him on a trip to London, where the Theosophical lodge, established in 1878 as the first official extra-American branch, faced difficulties. It transpired that the London Lodge, originally linked with the Arya Samaj movement, decided to break with them and appoint Sinnett as its new president. However, the former president he had replaced, the feminist, vegetarian, and medical doctor Anna Kingsford, vetoed Sinnett's election. In 1883, the lodge split into two rival factions. Olcott wished to re-establish order and unity among the British, so he sailed to Europe with Blavatsky. They arrived in Marseille in 1884. It is often said that this is how the founders of the original Theosophical Society introduced this school of thought in France.

However, as the historian Marie-José Delalande has ascertained,[49] the story is far more complicated. When they set foot on French soil, Blavatsky and Olcott were in fact greeted by French Theosophists: Dominique-Albert Courmes, a navy officer and *spirite* who had discovered Theosophical ideas during a stopover in Boston or New York and had been corresponding with Olcott since 1876, and Baron Spedalieri, a cabbalist who had also been in touch with Olcott and Blavatsky.

Spedalieri introduced Madame Blavatsky to Lady Caithness, also known as Duchesse de Pomar or Maria de Mariategui, who then lived in Nice. Lady Caithness was a wealthy aristocrat, a *spirite* and an occultist who tried to reconcile Catholicism with the ideas of Kardec and Blavatsky. She developed an intense devotion to Mary Stuart, the doomed Scottish monarch, who appeared to her and revealed herself as her guardian angel. Lady Caithness dedicated her life to religion and thought she would receive a Fourth Revelation from spiritual entities, which would crown the revelations of Moses, Jesus, and the 19th-century spirits.

Alexandra David-Néel frequented her mansion on the Avenue Wagram in Paris and left an interesting, if short and ironic, description. The house was a reproduction of Mary Stuart's Scottish castle at Holyrood. Amid the rich and heavy decorum Lady Caithness organized séances specifically dedicated to the martyred Catholic queen. Among the regulars at her salon was the famous astronomer Camille Flammarion, who became a Theosophist. It was Lady Caithness who in 1883 founded the first French Theosophical group, called *La Société Théosophique d'Orient et d'Occident*, even before she had met Helena Blavatsky. She had read *Isis Unveiled* and was convinced that the Orient could bring a lot to Western religions. When both ladies met, they affiliated the French society to the Adyar headquarters.

After her stay in Nice with Lady Caithness, Madame Blavatsky went to Paris and met people who had already absorbed her ideas through the *Revue spirite*, which had started publishing articles on Theosophy as early as 1876. Only nine months after the creation of the Theosophical Society in New York, Dominique-Albert Courmes published the first description of the Theosophists' ideas, which he attributed to Olcott rather than to Blavatsky. At first, Courmes was sceptical about these new ideas, because they contradicted the *spirites*' master, Allan Kardec. Indeed, Blavatsky considered that during séances, mediums were not in communication with the spirits of the dead but, rather, experienced the manifestation of "occult forces" that included both "elementals" (including natural but generally invisible beings, like fairies) and the individual psyches of the living persons witnessing paranormal phenomena. Later, in 1878, Courmes warmed to Blavatsky's new ideas, saying they might even complement Kardec's theories. The journal then published a 30-page supplement on Blavatsky's ideas to present the Theosophical Society to its readers. After that seminal publication, the *Revue spirite* between 1876 and 1882 offered 40 articles and numerous interleaves and notes on the Society's ideas and activities in India and on Madame Blavatsky's life, plus excerpts of correspondence between Theosophists disagreeing on various topics.

In 1882, however, this trend was blocked by some members of the reading committee who disapproved of Blavatsky's influence on the journal. They wanted to remain faithful to Kardec's ideas. Those who were impressed by the Theosophists' work, both on a doctrinal and a political level (with the creation of schools in India and the promotion of Hindu and Buddhist reform movements), created a small Theosophical group within the *Société scientifique d'études psychologiques*, dedicated to the study of spiritism and mesmerism. That small group continued to disseminate Theosophical ideas in the *Société*'s journal but soon had to stop for the same sectarian reasons. Therefore, when Madame Blavatsky and Colonel Olcott arrived in France in 1884, there was no longer any publication on Theosophy, but several *spirites* still eager to deepen their knowledge of Theosophical ideas.

They met, and several proposals were accepted. The director of the *Revue socialiste*, Benoît Malon, agreed to publish several articles by Madame Blavatsky. The director of *L'Antimatérialiste*, René Caillet, renamed his journal *Revue des Hautes Études* (1886-1887), which featured more articles by the Russian medium – but soon ceased publication. In 1887 one of these *spirites* inherited a family fortune and dedicated it to the creation of a new journal, *Le Lotus* 1888), the first French Theosophical journal, which bore the subtitle: *Revue des Hautes Études théosophiques tendant à rapprocher l'Orient et l'Occident* (Journal of High Theosophical Studies Seeking to Bring East and West Together). The journal lasted for two years and ceased publication after a clash between the editor and Papus over a critical note about his work. A new journal was founded by another aristocratic lady, titled *Le Lotus bleu* (1890), which is still published today. Alexandra David published some of her first writings in it. It is through those publications that Madame Blavatsky's ideas could reach a wider audience, which likely included Louise David.

Another important actor in the introduction of Theosophical ideas in France was the British socialist and feminist activist Annie Besant. Louise David probably met her at one of Besant's numerous conferences in Paris, hosted by Lady Caithness or the feminist, socialist, anticlerical Maria Deraismes, or at the *Société Géographique*, the Sorbonne, or the *Salle des Mathurins*, a salon in the 8th arrondissement that hosted conferences.

Annie Besant (1847-1933), assistant to the British MP, journalist and atheist Charles Bradlaugh, and an orator for the Fabian Society and the Marxist Social Democratic Federation, had been fascinated by *The Secret Doctrine* in 1888 and had publicly converted from Atheism to Theosophy. This was viewed as yet another scandal, as she had already shocked the British public with her rather explicit Malthusian brochures on birth control for London's East End population. She met with Blavatsky, trained with her for a few years before she died in 1891, and finally succeeded her as the thinking head of the Society. Besant was also instrumental in the decolonization of India.[50]

In 1886, a new French branch of the Theosophical Society was created. Its founders considered that Lady Caithness was not faithful enough to Madame Blavatsky's ideas and they wanted to establish a more authentic Theosophical Society in France. This branch was called *Isis* and was directed by Louis Dramart, a journalist and Republican who had been exiled for political reasons. The branch was quickly dissolved because of a dispute with Papus, and a new one was created in 1887, the *Hermès* branch, with Papus as one of its leaders, in direct relation with Adyar. Unfortunately, due to on-going rivalries, the *Hermès* branch also had to close and was replaced by a new one, *Ananta*. It is this branch Louise David joined around 1890 and which she depicts in *Le sortilège du mystère*. Later, this branch and others from other French regions gathered and were officially recognized as the French section of the Theosophical Society in 1899. France was the fourth country, after Great Britain, Sweden and the Netherlands, to have a Theosophical Section. The *Société théosophique de France* became a government-approved association in 1908.

In the late 1880s, with Alexandra David back home from her London trip, Mrs. Morgan wrote to her: "Since you enjoyed yourself at the 'Supreme Gnosis,' you will find a similar environment in Paris at the French headquarters of the Theosophical Society.

This Society is much more prestigious than the 'Supreme Gnosis.' It has ramifications in the entire world and its international headquarters are in India. I could, if you wish, introduce you to them and ask if there is any available room for you."[51] David-Néel writes that the prospect of living in the same kind of comfortable conditions in Paris delighted her and she accepted the offer. She was also curious, she says, to hear "new stories of the afterlife."

An American lady having just left, there was a room available for her. She presented herself to "Monsieur Jourdan" (E. J. Coulomb), the secretary of the Parisian Theosophical Lodge, on the Boulevard Saint Michel number 30.

She recounts her astonishment at the absence of a sign for any society. There was a large grocery store on the ground floor, with its produce displayed on the sidewalk – mountains of vegetables, poultry and other goods. It was nevertheless the correct address. She entered the corridor and asked the concierge if there was a society in the building. The latter, without even looking at her, replied that it was on the third floor. There, she found a sign that read: *"Société théosophique."* She rang the doorbell and "a minuscule woman, almost a dwarf" opened the door. There she found a narrow dark hall along which she could barely pull her suitcase. A man emerged and introduced himself as "Monsieur Jourdan, secretary of the French branch of the Theosophical Society."

She was hesitant, but the man confirmed that this small, dark, and humble apartment was indeed the French headquarters of the Theosophical Society. The main room contained a table cluttered with papers used as an office, a wicker chair, a writing desk stowed between the two windows overlooking the Boulevard, a chimney flanked with a red, worn-out armchair with a long backrest, a few chairs, and white bookshelves containing brand new books for sale.

When compared with the elegant and discreet London club that housed the Supreme Gnosis Society, this Parisian worker's home was rather disappointing. And so was her bedroom (with a mattress directly on the floor "to feel more Oriental") and the meals, composed of thin potato soup with soaked bread. To her dismay, there was no bathroom in the apartment, and she had to go to the public baths. Another woman would occupy the second guest bedroom. The Society had only two bedrooms for visitors, and the Coulomb family (husband, wife and four-year-old son) occupied the main part of the place. She writes: "My debut in the French occultist world was, at least from a materialistic point of view, rather bleak. I smiled at the thought of the pepper tea and sweet eggs I had for my first supper at the Supreme Gnosis."[52]

During that first memorable dinner, she and Mr Coulomb discussed the legitimacy of both the Supreme Gnosis and the Theosophical Society. According to Coulomb, "the Supreme Gnosis Society did not possess the tradition," they had "no lineal descendants." Alexandra David seemed to have no idea about the meaning of such a lineage, so he explained to her that the Theosophical Society received its knowledge from "entities that were about to populate the earth and were still in [sic] the moon." Some of the Theosophical Society's members "who have attained a very high degree of evolution" have "contemplated that fact," and let the other members know about their discoveries.[53] As he spoke, Coulomb's face looked strangely absorbed, his eyes staring into space. Then, he took on a condescending air and explained to her: "Certain transcendental entities which used to inhabit the moon consciously proceeded to their change of planets. Did they dematerialize the substance of their form to rematerialize it later when they reached their new home, or was this substance made of so subtle an essence that it could, like a wave, travel into space?

Who knows? ...Some inferior forms of life then existed on Earth, and the highly evolved Lunars united with them."

Alexandra David reminded him of a quote from *Genesis*, VI, 2: "The sons of God saw the daughters of men and found them beautiful. They united with them," to which the secretary replied: "Yes, yes. There are esoteric data to collect in the Bible for those capable of discovering them... Some of those individualities, in their present terrestrial form, remember the Lunars, their friends or parents who emigrated with them and whom they can recognize. Hence the friendly associations produced by those antique affinities. Several of our spiritual Masters are thus linked with one another by the power of intellectual or loving relationships, or by that of the spiritual work they started together billions of centuries ago and are still undertaking today."[54]

It seems that this insistence on extra-terrestrials within the French Theosophical Lodge did not satisfy her intellectual standards. She could certainly accept that "hidden masters" lived in the East whose goal it was to guide humanity on its path to spiritual and earthly accomplishment, but the faith in the "Lunars" that Coulomb professed was probably too much for her. However, it is likely that she remained a member of the Theosophical Society because it provided an international network of like-minded people ready to assist her on trips abroad, especially in India, and because it allowed her to discover Asian languages, beliefs and practices.

But in a contorted way she quickly started to question these premises. In fact, the two main procedures taught by Coulomb, who was the head of a small Parisian community of devotees, were original hybrid meditative practices based on the reading of the *Bhagavad-Gîta* in Sanskrit. The reading was not performed in an exoteric or esoteric way (learning the literal or hidden meaning of the text) but was based on a physical approach – the third meaning of the cathedral metaphor, according to which sounds have a direct effect on practitioners' bodies.

The first practice taught by Coulomb was the study of the *Bhagavad-Gîta* both in Sanskrit and in French translation. Those study sessions, which happened late at night, actually entailed the loud and musical pronunciation of Sanskrit syllables, supposed to touch "the internal ear and the spiritual eyes" with their "vibrations." Those vibrations were thought to lead the practitioner, touched in his or her internal, or "astral," body, to an altered state of consciousness that facilitated the contemplation of other realities on higher spiritual levels. The French translation, according to the practitioners Alexandra David met, were only useful to beginners, in other words, unimportant.[55]

This practice is in tune with the advice Madame Blavatsky gives in *Secret Instructions to Probators of an Esoteric Occult School* and *The Voice of Silence*,[56] where she establishes a series of correspondences between sounds, colors, ideas, letters and musical notes, while emphasizing the physical power of Hindu and Buddhist mantras on the practitioner's mind. It is interesting to note that this understanding of sacred scriptures in terms of "vibrations" still exists today at Buddhist centres, where the Tibetan language plays the exact same role as Sanskrit did in the late 19th century.

The second practice taught by Coulomb, very popular among 19th-century esoteric groups, was "astral projection" or "etheric travel." This approach was based on the Neo-Platonic premise that each being has several bodies that range from the most material to the most ethereal. One of these, called the astral body, was believed to be an intermediate source of light that links the physical body to the "Rational Soul" or "Great Intellect" – i.e., God, understood in a pantheistic way. The astral body is thus an occultist name for the Platonic notion of soul. According to Neo-Platonic traditions, the astral body belongs to an astral plane in which other forms of life evolve, such as angels, demons and spirits. Convinced that it was possible to take control of one's own astral bodies, the Theosophists – as well as adepts of Rosicrucianism and the Golden Dawn, the Theosophical Society's main competitors in the late 19th century – believed they could make contact with these parallel universes and retrieve information and personal messages from the ethereal beings. Practitioners would then describe their travels to heavens, hells, the astrological spheres, and other planets.

Although the practice is well established, what is interesting here is the innovation introduced by the Theosophists – trance-like states were not generated by drugs or lack of sleep or food, but by the reading of a Sanskrit text. The young and insightful Alexandra David, however, thought there must be more to the *Bhagavad-Gîta* than mere "etheric vibrations," so she decided to seek knowledge from other Orientalists of the time, scholars from the Sorbonne and the Collège de France. She was not convinced by the "travels" occultist colleagues claimed to have experienced through Sanskrit phonemes, and she writes that, apart from Coulomb and one or two others, nobody else was convinced, either.[57]

Alexandra David became increasingly sceptical of the Theosophists' teachings but remained a member throughout her life and retained many of their tropisms – an interest in altered states of consciousness and unexplained extraordinary faculties (she would later write about the Tibetan lamas' superpowers, notably their ability to create *tulpas*, which she describes using the occultists' vocabulary as "etheric doubles"), a search for Asian "initiates," and an interest in Eastern sacred texts.

In fact, she seemed to have followed the trail of her personal model and teacher, Annie Besant, who was gaining authority within the European and Eastern Theosophical Society after Madame Blavatsky's death in 1891 and was also pursuing political and feminist goals. Through Besant and her father's connections in socialist and anarchist movements, Alexandra David launched a new career in politics, which seemed to have surpassed her occultist leanings. She remained interested in occult phenomena, as her subsequent books on Hinduism and Tibetan Buddhism suggest, but she was keen to learn more about the cultural contexts in which those two religions emerged.

She was becoming more an ethnographer (an "Orientalist journalist," as she put it) than a conventional occultist absorbed in imaginary travels. She wanted to journey to the Orient in the flesh rather than in dreams and meet "mahatmas" in person. In a way, the Theosophical Society served as a bridge in David-Néel's intellectual trajectory. It led her from Gnosticism to Asian religions, from the role of spiritual seeker to that of the traveller and ethnologist, and from an occult scene still dominated by male figures to one of the first women-only radical political clubs.

3

A Buddhist in *Fin-de-Siècle* Paris

> *The scandal increased when Pécuchet declared that he liked Buddhism just as much.*
> *The priest burst out laughing: "Ha, Ha! Buddhism!"*
> *Madame de Noaris threw up her arms: "Buddhism!"*
> *"What... Buddhism!" the count repeated.*
> *"Do you know about it?" Pécuchet said to Mr. Jeufroy, who was confused. "Very well, listen to this! Buddhism recognized the vanity of earthly things better and earlier than Christianity. Its practices are austere, its faithful more numerous than all Christians put together and, as for the Incarnation, Vishnu did not have one, but nine! So, judge from that!"*
> *"Travelers' lies," said Madame de Noaris.*
> *"Supported by Freemasons," added the curé.*
>
> **Gustave Flaubert, *Bouvard et Pécuchet*, 1881**

Did Alexandra David-Néel ever Claim to be a Buddhist?

According to the legend, Alexandra David converted to Buddhism while standing in front of a monumental Buddha statue at the recently built Guimet Museum in Paris. This aesthetic experience, combined with her lifelong spiritual quest, allegedly had a profound influence on her thought and behavior, naturally leading her to Tibet where she supposedly found what she had always been seeking.

The story is obviously simplistic. What did she really discover at the Guimet Museum? Was it the only place in Paris where Buddhism was presented to the public? Didn't she first hear about the Buddha and his teachings in the spiritualist circles she frequented? Granted that she travelled to Tibet to receive teachings from lamas, that she wrote extensively about Buddhism and was called a Buddhist by her entourage, but are we sure that she really identified herself as a Buddhist? And if that was the case, what did she mean by the term?

Several documents attest to Louise David's early interest in Buddhism. We know she would have started researching the subject in 1892, while an active and enthusiastic member of the Theosophical Society. In 1893, she wrote an article in response to a charismatic French orientalist, Léon de Rosny, about the meaning of esotericism in Buddhism and the possible existence of Buddhist mahatmas. This is the first article on Buddhism we have by Louise David, who signed with her initiate's name, Mitra – "friend" in Sanskrit, but with a similar ring to the Mithra of Roman mystery cults.

In 1895 she published another article titled *Notes sur le Bouddhisme* (Notes on Buddhism) in a socialist newspaper. In it she states that "All the Buddha's law and prescriptions can be summed up in this word: Knowledge," which sounds like a Gnostic rendering of the Buddhist doctrine. She also adds: "After centuries of depressing [Christian] predications, of resignation and of renunciation, new voices are rising today that firmly proclaim each being's imprescriptible right to happiness." Those voices, she writes, are "none other than an echo of the Buddha's own words: Every suffering is a disorder." This certainly echoes her parallel socialist activities.

In 1901 another article came out, *Un mot sur le Bouddhisme* (A Word on Buddhism), in a sociological and ethnological journal.[58] This article explains why Buddhism and Christianity are antithetical, with a phrasing that suggests that the former is evidently superior to the latter. In 1909, she published, under the name of Alexandra David, an article titled *Quelques écrivains bouddhistes contemporains* (A few contemporary Buddhist writers) in the prestigious literary journal, *Le Mercure de France*. In it she shares her enthusiasm for the social activism endorsed by several Western converts and Asian reformers, tending to confirm the political leanings she wanted to give Buddhism.

These articles, tracking the evolution of her model of Buddhism from occultist to revolutionary, were just part of her vast literary output. From the 1890s to the 1910s she published articles on social and political issues, feminism, eugenics, Asian religious doctrines and practices, Chinese philosophers, and theoretical views on cultural and religious diversity. She also wrote two feminist novels and several Theosophical papers.[59] From this list of publications Buddhism appears to be but one of several intellectual preoccupations, albeit a cherished one.

The first hints of David-Néel's clear identification of herself as a Buddhist seem to emerge in her writings between 1909 and 1912. In a letter she wrote in 1909 to a university professor she had befriended but who was later disappointed with her rejection of Christianity, she explains: "The Gospel seemed small compared to Hindu philosophy… in it I saw a doctrine good enough for Galilean fishermen, but incapable of retaining an intellectual's attention… I believe in the superiority of the Buddha's philosophical teachings over those of Jesus. Buddhism took over my brain, and I live only through the latter."

However, as the expression "Hindu philosophy" indicates, she seemed to conceive of Buddhism as a kind of Hindu school: its aim, she writes, is to "lead to the mystical union described in the *Bhagavad Gita*."⁶⁰ At this point in her intellectual journey there was apparently no major difference in her understanding of Buddhism and Hinduism. The Buddha was a sophisticated "Hindu philosopher" who stood out among other thinkers for his indifference towards gods and metaphysical questions and for his exclusive focus on the eradication of suffering. For these reasons he particularly appealed to her.

Two years later, in a letter to her husband from India, she positively describes herself as a Buddhist and makes a clear distinction between her faith and that of the Hindu people she lived with, who she thinks wrongly believe in gods. She also told her husband she taught Buddhism to a group of young Hindus.⁶¹ So David-Néel not only considered herself a Buddhist, she also took on the role of a Buddhist teacher.

A year later, in 1912, she published an article in *Le Mercure de France* about her encounter with the 13th Dalai Lama in Kalimpong. She explains that she convinced "the Lamaist Pope" to meet a European woman by saying she came to speak with him not as a simple Westerner but as his coreligionist.⁶² Further evidence of David-Néel's self-identification as a Buddhist is found in an unpublished text probably written in 1913 or 1914. The text, titled *Au Pays du Bouddha* (In the Buddha's Land), affirms that her trips to India and Nepal were Buddhist pilgrimages: "I came here – why should I hide this – on a pilgrimage motivated by the memory of a venerated Master."⁶³

It is, therefore, clearly established that as early as 1911 (if not before) David-Néel thought of herself as a Buddhist and did not hesitate to teach other people what she knew about Buddhism. It had been one of the foci of her intellectual curiosity since the early 1890s and eventually became a point of faith. The obvious question now is: how did she become a Buddhist, where did her grasp of Buddhism originate?

Discussing Buddhist Esotericism with Léon de Rosny

The first article Louise David wrote about Buddhism is doubtless her response to Léon de Rosny, published in the French Theosophical journal *Le Lotus bleu* in 1893. The discussion between the young Theosophist and the established scholar followed a dispute that unfolded in England the same year. Madame Blavatsky (who died in 1891) had been accused by the eminent scholar Max Müller of disseminating erroneous and foolish ideas about Eastern religions.[64] Her inability to read Sanskrit and questions about the veracity of her alleged sources, the mahatmas, were at the centre of the debate. Could one pretend to know ancient Indian traditions without being able to read Sanskrit or Pali texts? Was it enough to claim access to mysterious great masters to be a legitimate teacher of Oriental doctrines? Did one not need to learn Buddhism from Sanskrit texts since, contrary to Hinduism, Buddhism had disappeared from India centuries ago? In other words, was it reasonable to assume that a secret oral transmission had guaranteed a direct and unspoiled transmission from the Buddha himself to a handful of initiates?

Max Müller clearly considered this perception nonsensical and regretted that Blavatsky had given the impression that Indian Buddhism was no different from her secret doctrine. According to Léon de Rosny (1837-1914), an eminent though eccentric ethnologist and linguist and one of the first scholars of the Japanese language in France, Indian Buddhism never was, nor ever intended to be, "a mysterious religion." Knowing what he knew about how Tibetans practiced Buddhism ("a ridiculous caricature of the great doctrine of the Buddha Shakyamuni"), he wrote that there was little chance that Blavatsky's mahatmas really existed.

However, de Rosny did not fully agree with Max Müller on his point that Sanskrit and Pali texts were the only way to learn what Buddhism really is about: "It is not by peeling Sanskrit roots that one will succeed in taking advantage of the sublime perceptions that made the Buddha one of the most brilliant meteors of the thinking part of humanity. The works of Orientalism have brought us, it is true, valuable instruments of study, but they have spread about Buddhism the most obscure, the most contradictory ideas. It is now up to thinkers to enter the arena and to clean the stables of Augias where professional scholars allow themselves, perhaps a little too shamelessly, to deposit rubbish."[65]

By "thinkers" de Rosny meant people like himself, for he was not only an ethnologist and linguist but also a philosopher. Indeed, de Rosny had developed a new doctrine he called "consciential method" or "exactivist philosophy," a kind of spiritualist positivism that was later reformulated and promoted by Henri Bergson.[66] He notably used this method to elaborate a synthesis of Buddhism, Christianity and Positivism, which he called "Eclectic Buddhism."[67]

Louise David had apparently pondered the question of esoteric Buddhism and decided to write a response to de Rosny's piece. She introduced the "ambientist" argument (also called the "theory of climates"), an 18th-century materialistic theory about the emergence of cultural variations.[68] The best way to understand the supernatural and magical elements found in Buddhist texts, she writes, is not to presume the existence of hidden great masters who possess the secret knowledge to decipher their true meaning, but to attribute their emergence to the physical environment in which the authors of those stories lived.

True to her habit of interpreting symbols through an analysis of the physical context from which they grew (the third way to look at a temple, as noted), Louise David explains that Buddhist esotericism was caused by, and thus should be explained in terms of, the Indian climate and landscape. She writes: "Open the *Lalita Vistara* or the *Kandjour* and you will be amazed at one of those gigantic dreams, as India alone could have made, in the midst of its liana-filled forests full of immense flowers, under its fiery sky. It is in this imaginative overflow that one must seek esotericism."[69]

The most important secrets of Eastern religious traditions, she adds, are of another kind. They are not connected to "golden and illuminated temples" or "clergies and ceremonies," which "all the peoples who preceded us over the ages and those who will follow us for centuries" have always controlled and always will. This, she says, and all "the symbols, parables, and allegories" are only good for "the crowd," which cannot understand "high philosophical conceptions." She agrees with Madame Blavatsky that these ideas are only revealed by great sages to a handful of chosen and tested disciples endowed with "superior minds."

But what those masters transmit to disciples does not result from deciphering complicated symbols – these should simply be abandoned, not interpreted. What masters secretly transmit from one generation to the next is nothing less than the ultimate truth about the world. And this truth appears when ignorance, another name for esotericism, has been vanquished by knowledge.

Mitra is thus a surprising occultist, here refuting any significance to symbolic expression. Her approach is unquestionably positivist. She reasons that esotericism is not a sophisticated language one learns from a spiritual master; it is just another name for religion or superstition, those irrational beliefs and practices reserved for the uneducated, foolish crowd. Buddhism does have a secret dimension, however: "high philosophical conceptions" reserved for an intellectual elite. Therefore, she says, Max Müller was wrong to claim that only the study of Sanskrit texts could teach us what Buddhism really is about. One should take seriously the possibility that mahatmas, the intellectual elite of mankind, really exist and are the repositories of the Buddha's original teachings. To gain a clearer idea of what these original teachings really were, it was thus essential to travel to Asia and hear them directly from Buddhist intellectuals.

Louise David's position regarding Buddhist esotericism is thus a compromise between de Rosny's view (one should look for "high philosophy" in any religious doctrine, with all the metaphysical and mythological details just biproducts of the physical environment) and Madame Blavatsky's theory (mahatmas exist, superior beings who received the truth orally from older generations, but they certainly are not those described by the founder of the Theosophical Society). Her leap of originality over both authors is to speculate that real Asian sages could teach Europeans the great secrets of life. Madame Blavatsky pretended to derive her doctrine from the direct teachings of fictitious characters, while de Rosny thought it was up to European thinkers (himself specifically) to revive a synthesized version of the Buddha's real teachings. Both attitudes precluded any serious dialogue with Asian Buddhists.

Louise David's new understanding of Oriental traditions prompted her to abandon the pure domain of literature (she had published both fiction and philosophy) to enter the discipline of ethnography, albeit from a Theosophical viewpoint. For Louise David was still the initiate Mitra; what she wanted to do in Asia was find the real, intellectual mahatmas that Madame Blavatsky had concealed behind her imaginary esoteric creatures.

Eclectic Buddhism and Official Buddhism

Although she never mentioned him in her books, it seems that Léon de Rosny played a key role in Louise David's intellectual development. First, we have the 1893 article in which she engages with him and agrees about almost everything – the pre-eminence of philosophical conceptions over all kinds of religiosity (including esotericism), the anthropological theory of climates, and the inadequacy of Sanskrit studies to expedite the discovery of Buddhism. Then we can also consider evidence that they personally knew each other.

In the "blue notebook" kept in her archives, which contains notes written toward the end of her life for an unfinished autobiography, we find two interesting clues. First, she writes that she "started a Theosophical correspondence with Jacques Tasset, Léon Weiskop, and Vittoria Cremer" in 1892. Jacques Tasset was, in fact, not only a Theosophist but also a disciple of de Rosny's.[70] We know from David-Néel's correspondence with her husband that Tasset had been an important friend of hers. As proof of their friendship, he brought her a little Buddha statue from Japan, where he often travelled. This is the statue she is holding with both hands and showing off as a precious relic in the photograph showing her dressed as some kind of medieval penitent.[71] We may reasonably infer that Jacques Tasset introduced her to his master, Léon de Rosny, to his Eclectic School, and perhaps also to Buddhism. The second clue we get from the blue notebook is an entry confirming she "went to see de Rosny" in 1901. Furthermore, she had a copy of *Eclectic Buddhism* in her library.

What exactly was de Rosny's Eclectic Buddhism and what sort of impact did this book have on the French public? According to Jules Bois, a contemporary writer and journalist specializing in occultism,[72] de Rosny was the leader of one of the two camps of Parisian Buddhists. Indeed, according to Bois, there were "at least ten thousand adepts" in Paris, split into two categories: "the scholars" and "the worried souls." The first group was led by "official scientists, like those of the Guimet Museum," the second was a kind of sect gathered around Léon de Rosny. Jules Bois describes de Rosny as "an apostle" who worked "at an immense desk resembling a craftsman's table" in "a wooden and painted circular study… dressed with messianic simplicity." He reminded him of Tolstoy.

Léon de Rosny confessed to Jules Bois that he regretted having "so many enemies" in academia who reproached him for not behaving like a scholar while projecting himself as a religious master. De Rosny, however, found it natural to attract young people with questions about life, just as Renan had done in the past. He also claimed to be uninterested in what he called "Logomachy," that is, scholarly or intellectual debates. What counts, he said, is "universal love," and he believed that historical knowledge had no value whatsoever. Only timeless ideas were important: "Erudition, texts, I do not care. I take my good where I find it, and I care little that my ideas belong less to the Buddha than to Voltaire, Rousseau, or Hegel. I bother as much about history as I do about doormen's gossip. Now, [philosophical] systems belong no more to Plato than to Jesus or Laozi. We have made such remarkable progress… The true Gospels, for example, reside much more in our memory than in the texts. And it may happen that a cabbie knows much more about Buddhism than Max Müller, who ignores everything except Sanskrit."[73]

The sort of Buddhism a cabbie could understand better than the most erudite scholars is described in *Eclectic Buddhism*. It is "the substance that can be derived from Buddhism, as it results from the work of ages and from the progress that was made necessary by critical thought" – in other words, Buddhism read in the light of the ideology of progress.[74] De Rosny has extracted this "from the best doctrines of old Asia" in order to "take advantage of them for the study of the problem of Life and Destiny," to "learn what Buddhism could offer us, not only to examine, under a favourable light, the obscure question of our origins and ends, but also to determine the moral and intellectual law of our conduct on this earth."[75]

Eclectic Buddhism, then, is a hybrid doctrine that mixes Positivism, Buddhism and Christianity. It is quite close to the definition Henry Steel Olcott had given of Buddhism a decade before: its essence is "self-culture and universal love," it imposes no irrational beliefs and is compatible with the latest state of scientific knowledge.[76] De Rosny mentions Olcott's *Buddhist Catechism* several times in his footnotes.

However, Eclectic Buddhism is more philosophical and more abstract in its formulation. Surprisingly, it also rejects some of the new dogmas about Buddhism expounded in the second half of the 19th century. Notably, de Rosny did not consider the Buddha to be an atheist; he simply did not bother to define what God really is. To conclude from his absence of "logomachy" about God that the Buddha rejected this notion is a mistake too many scholars make. According to de Rosny, the Buddha did believe in God – but not in an anthropomorphic God. His reasoning is an implicit syllogism: "The most gigantic hypothesis ever formulated by the human mind is most probably the idea of God."[77] Shakyamuni was one of the most sophisticated thinkers in history, therefore he cannot have concluded that God does not exist.[78]

Another original feature is the value de Rosny attributes to suffering. Whereas most Buddhist modernists claim the Buddha's most interesting contribution was his revelation of the Four Noble Truths and his condemnation of suffering, de Rosny thinks that those truths are only a tiny and superficial part of his teachings. According to the same kind of syllogism – which might be part of his "consciential method" – the Buddha cannot have condemned suffering since suffering is "the spur of moral rectification" and "the work of God," and the Buddha was a superior mind who could not ignore this reality. His real teachings, de Rosny claims, consisted in other truths: "We can triumph over every obstacle through meditative research coupled with moral rectification,"[79] the most important practice is "to love all creatures,"[80] the second is to "look for Knowledge,"[81] and the ultimate goal of human life, and of humanity in general, is to reach perfection, which is essentially moral.[82] Yet, as Jules Bois clearly indicated, while de Rosny's doctrine attracted disciples, it was not well received by other scholars, who advocated a more academic approach to Buddhism.

Many of these scholars, who represented the official understanding of Buddhism in France, started collaborating with

Émile Guimet on his pedagogical project around 1890. Guimet[83] was the son and heir of a scientist and entrepreneur who made his fortune with the invention of a chemical dye. His father was also a Saint-Simonian and educated his child according to the values of this school of thought. Saint-Simonianism was a social, political and religious movement, emerging in the first half of the 19th century, based on the teachings of Henri de Rouvroy, Comte de Saint-Simon (1750-1825), a businessman and political theorist. Saint-Simon believed that progress must reflect what he called "industrialism." According to this doctrine, the working class must receive a decent salary and other social benefits so that society not only becomes efficiently industrialized but also benefits from each person's wellbeing. The goal is to build a perfectly harmonized and happy society where everyone's needs are fulfilled. Saint-Simonianism had a major influence on socialism, anarchism and communism.

Like his father, who introduced social services and educational activities for his factories' workers, Émile Guimet decided to contribute to the public's intellectual growth through the foundation of a new museum dedicated to the history of religions. The museum was finally established in Paris on the Place d'Iéna in 1889, after years of waiting and political pressure. Some members of Parliament objected to the creation of a museum dedicated to "the propagation of superstitions," and the Minister of Instruction, who had agreed to the project and proposed substantial financial support, almost cancelled his agreement with Guimet. The idea of a "temple-museum" was unbearable to many politicians. The project was saved by the intervention of the socialist member of Parliament Alexandre Millerand (who became the French President in 1920), who said: "Putting the past of disappeared religions before the public's eye is the best way to wage an effective war against the religions of today."[84]

The study of Buddhism, whether in Léon de Rosny's school or in official circles, was apparently also motivated by the intention to offer an alternative to the historic and still dominant religion, Catholicism. The success of Buddhism in Parisian intellectual circles and the interest it represented for Louise David should be viewed in this polemical context.

Guimet was an aesthete who had a passion for the arts, music, and travel. He was a musician and composer, fond of writing, and had been taught to appreciate the arts by his mother, a professional painter. He developed a particular taste for Egyptology, and travelled around the world, particularly in Egypt (1865-1866), India, China, Japan and America (1876-1877). From his travels, he brought home an enormous quantity of objects, including Egyptian steles, statues, sarcophagi, mummies, funerary figurines, amulets and papyrus, Buddha statues of all sizes, ritual objects, stupas, Chinese and Japanese paintings, etc.

He also published illustrated travel accounts such as *Croquis égyptiens: journal d'un touriste* (Egyptian Sketches: a Tourist's Diary, 1867), *Promenades japonaises* (Japanese Promenades, 1878-1880), and *Huit jours aux Indes* (Eight Days in India, 1889). His aim was to make his objects available to the public so that, just as he did during his travels, they could reflect on the evolution and diversity of religious thought. He wanted to "make the objects talk" and explain their civilizations to the public. Based on his observations at the Boulaq museum in Egypt and the Centennial Exposition in Philadelphia in 1876, he organised his collections according to the latest standards – a written description outlined the object's provenance and function and its meaning and significance in terms of the broader culture from which it came.

Guimet quickly organized public conferences and professional congresses, participated in the activities of several learned societies, published catalogues, official reports and monographs, and also funded a scholarly journal called *Revue d'histoire des religions* (Journal of the History of Religions), which started in 1879 with contributions from scholars of the Collège de France. One of his most original ideas was to show Buddhist ceremonies to the public.

Three ceremonies were organized at the Guimet Museum during the decade – in 1891, 1893 and 1898.[85] On February 21, 1891, two Japanese priests from the Jōdo Shin-shū (Pure Land) school, Ryōtai Koizumi and Hōgen Yoshitsura, celebrated the Hōonko-shiki (memorial service of the school's founder, Shinran Shōnin) in the circular library of the museum, converted into a temple for the occasion. The two priests arrived in Marseille on January 29 and took the train to Paris, where they visited the Guimet Museum on February 1 and 2. They were then introduced to Guimet himself. The priests were so enthusiastic about the place that they asked permission to perform a ritual, which, of course, Guimet immediately granted.

The performance was an unprecedented Parisian attraction. It was the perfect occasion to apply Guimet's approach to religion: "When one really wishes to appreciate the ancient or exotic civilizations that were the object of my preoccupations, one needs to abstract oneself from one's own beliefs, to strip ready-made ideas given by one's education or environment... It is necessary to travel, to touch the believer, to talk to him, to watch him act."[86]

The ritual was performed in front of a statue of Amida and a representation of Shinran and included all the traditional elements: praise, confessions, offerings, invocations, dedication of merit to all living beings. A hundred people were invited, including high-level Parisian celebrities: the representative of the French Republic, several ministers, including Jules Ferry, the fiercely anticlerical former Minister of Instruction and Prime Minister, members of foreign embassies, artists, painters (Edgar Degas), sculptors (Albert Bartholomé), writers, and amateurs of "japonisme" including the anticlerical member of Parliament

Georges Clémenceau (future Prime Minister and War Minister), who declared to a journalist that there was no contradiction in his participating in a religious ceremony, "since he was a Buddhist."

The second performance took place on November 13, 1893, "in honour of all the buddhas and bodhisattvas." It was led by Hōryu Toki, a Shingon priest who was then visiting Europe after participating in the Parliament of World's Religion in Chicago (September 11-27, 1893).[87] The ritual was presented to the public as very special, since the monk belonged to an "esoteric sect." It also attracted many personalities, including Georges Clémenceau and Léon Bourgeois, Minister of the Interior and future President of the Senate, Louis Pasteur and other scientists, Léon de Rosny and other people interested in Japan, artists, journalists and businessmen.

The third ceremony took place on June 27, 1898 and was performed by a Mongolian monk, Agvan Dorzhiev, who had initially come to Paris for political reasons.[88] Dorzhiev had visited a French scientist of Russian origin, Joseph Deniker, with whom he discussed Buddhism and the French Buddhists. Deniker told him about Guimet's art collection, and they went to see the museum together. Dorzhiev met with Guimet, who asked him to perform a ritual from his school. He did so in the presence of approximately two hundred people, among them Clémenceau and a certain "Alexandra" who strongly impressed Dorzhiev: "Although she was born a woman, she had personally trained herself in wisdom."[89]

There is no doubt that Alexandra David frequented the Guimet Museum. In one of her books, she writes that her vocation as an orientalist was born there: "In those times, the Guimet Museum was a temple. This is how it stands now, in my memory. I see a large stone staircase rising between walls covered with frescoes. As you climbed the steps, you successively encountered a haughty Brahmin pouring an offering into the sacred fire; Buddhist monks dressed in yellow togas begging for their daily food, a bowl in hand; a Japanese temple standing on a promontory to which an alley lined with cherry blossoms, beyond a red torii gate, led. Other characters, other landscapes from Asia solicited the pilgrim's attention that climbed up to the mystery of the Orient. At the top of the stairs, the "holy of holies" appeared as a dark antrum. Through a heavy grid that forbade any access, one got a glimpse of a rotunda with walls entirely filled with books. Dominating the library from high above, a giant Buddha sat, solitary, lost in his meditations… In this little room, mute calls emerged from the pages that one browsed. India, China, Japan, all the places in the world that start beyond Suez sought readers… Vocations were born… Mine was born there. So was the Guimet Museum when I was twenty years old."[90]

How did she first discover this place? In an interview she gave at the end of her life,[91] David-Néel said that, while at the Theosophical Society, she met "a Korean exile who worked at the Guimet Museum" and who brought her there. It was at the beginning of her Theosophical career, so this must have been late 1892 or early 1893.

We do not exactly know, however, what she read or learned there, but the contents of her personal library, kept in Digne, give us some indication. Among the French books she probably read in the 1890s are several volumes of the Guimet Museum's annals, Soubhadra Bhikshou's *Catéchisme bouddhique* (1888), Léon de Milloué's *Le bouddhisme dans le monde* (1893), Victor Barrucand's *Bouddhisme* (1893), and Léon de Rosny's *Bouddhisme éclectique* (1894). She also possessed, from the same period but in English: Alfred Sinnett's *Esoteric Buddhism* (1883), W. Rockhill's *Udānavarga From the Buddhist Canon* (1883), Paul Carus' *The Gospel of Buddha* (1894) and *The Dharma or the Religion of Enlightenment* (1898), and Mabel Bode's *Women Leaders of the Buddhist Reformation* (1892). The list, of course, is not exhaustive, as she probably read many other books without purchasing them.

We also know that she took a few lessons in Sanskrit, as an auditor at the Sorbonne, probably in 1893.[92]

Nonetheless, the interesting variety of sources she used to build her knowledge of Buddhism points in several directions: Buddhism as a progressive esoteric or philosophical doctrine (Sinnett, de Rosny), Buddhism as an exotic religion (Guimet's annals), Buddhism as a feminist endeavour (Bode), Buddhism as the "new religion of science" (Carus, Olcott translated by "Soubhadra Bhikshou," apparently an anonymous French occultist author), Buddhism as a morally advanced religion that can be compared to Christianity (de Milloué), Buddhism as a revolutionary enterprise (Barrucand, a socialist writer). The following decade, as we shall see, attests to her choice in favor of the last option.

What clearly appears as the immediate result of those readings is her radical condemnation of any kind of rapprochement between Buddhism and Christianity. She thought a fundamental misinterpretation by scholars and other intellectuals was exposed by their attempt to draw positive parallels between Buddhism and Christianity. It is senseless, she writes, to claim that Buddhism and Christianity share the same kind of approach to life and the same moral values. On the contrary, they are radically opposed and that is precisely why Buddhism is so superior.

At the very beginning of her 1895 article, *Notes sur le bouddhisme*, she writes: "Speaking of Buddhism, we easily imagine, under the Eastern skies, pagodas peopled with bizarre idols, before which processions of bonzes with dazzling robes take place, just as the word 'Christianity' arouses ideas of cathedrals, of Madonnas surrounded by candles, and priestly black robes in the dim light of confessionals. From there one concludes that, even in its very form, Christianity – or rather Catholicism – is one and the same as Buddhism. However, nothing is more wrong… There is an abyss between the philosophy attributed to prince Siddartha (Shakyamuni Buddha) and the speeches attributes to Jesus."[93]

The main difference between the two traditions revolves around the notion of pain. According to Mitra, the Buddha was profoundly shocked by suffering and decided to find a rational way to eradicate it, whereas Christianity gave it an "irrational" (i.e., altruistic) and unfair meaning: "Buddhist philosophy was born from witnessing human suffering, that suffering that does not move us anymore, for we are so used to seeing it everywhere, and that was the object of the Buddha's constant meditations. Contrary to religions that consecrate suffering by making it meritorious or by seeing it as the will of a god that should be accepted without a murmur; instead of, finally, preaching resignation to our ills, the Buddha, penetrated with compassion for his brothers, told himself that it was necessary to find the cause of suffering, and once this cause was known, to destroy it." And, she says, "the cause of suffering is ignorance" (without identifying what this ignorance is).[94]

She was therefore totally opposed to de Rosny's understanding of suffering. The second main difference between Buddhism and Christianity is the egalitarian view of humanity that she attributes to the former and seems to deny to the latter. She writes: "So proud is this philosophy that considers every living beings of *Samsara* (the circle of existences) as equivalent. Gods, men, animals, plants, beings of all kinds, inhabitants of all worlds, all manifestations of life have the same value. No superiors, no inferiors, no other link than those of universal fraternity."[95]

The only resemblance between the two traditions is the religious degradation that afflicted the founder's initial doctrines. The Buddha's philosophy was "so uncomplicated" that "the oriental mind" – which due to the Indian climate is prone to invent exuberant beliefs – turned it into complex doctrines, rituals and hierarchies. That is how the Chinese and Japanese religions came to life, wrongly claiming the name Buddhism for themselves.

Because the Buddha's disciples added cranky ideas of their own to the pure original teachings of their master, powerful institutions were established, in the exact same way that Jesus' teachings were corrupted by the founders of the Church.

"If one considers the hierarchy, the clergy, the ceremonies, etc.," she writes, "one is obliged to recognize that, on this ground, it is not only Buddhism and Catholicism that can be compared, but all official religions, Brahmanism, Islamism, etc." Even the Protestants who revolted against the Catholic Church followed its model when they established themselves in England. Mitra gives a universal explanation to this phenomenon: "This is a curious fact that despite the difference in dogmas, the organization is the same in Constantinople, Moscow, Rome, or Lhasa... Why is that? Because people are and have always been kept on a leash, because civil and religious hierarchies are the two most efficient instruments of authority, this monster that is now even more formidable since it is impersonal, everyone being part of it and being crushed by oneself."[96]

In her 1901 article, *Un mot sur le bouddhisme*,[97] she makes similar comments about what she feels has become the official view of Buddhism. She writes that, either from the study of texts or from observations of Buddhist practices in Asia, most people agree on the resemblance between Buddhism and Christianity. She thinks that reducing an exotic tradition to what we already know and believe in is a simplistic and narcissistic mistake – what today we call ethnocentrism. She develops the same arguments about the different conceptions of suffering in the two traditions but adds further derogatory descriptions of Christianity: Siddhartha was "a prince, the king's son" motivated to act by pure compassion for the suffering beings he encountered on his way, whereas Jesus was but "a craftsman impelled to preaching by a faith, as ardent as it was irrational, in the Master of the skies and earth…"

The Buddha, on the other hand, was a rational and sensible person who belonged to the Aryan race and shared its superior beliefs. Indeed, an important point she raises as a positive argument in favor of Buddhism is its "materialist philosophy, in the highest sense of the word." She writes: "Educated by scholars, understanding the profound cosmological system of the Aryans under the layers of symbols, Siddhartha is a materialist philosopher in the highest sense of the word. He adores nothing, he invokes no celestial being. He does not pray, he meditates; he is not a supplicating devotee – he is a thinker."[98]

Knowing what those two figures were – one a hysteric, the other a sage – it is easy to understand, she writes, why those two systems have absolutely nothing in common. The Buddha's doctrine is entirely "rational," that is, intellectual and pragmatic. It is based on knowledge and reflection (rather than on faith and sentiment) and should lead to practical benefits for individuals and society (instead of answering fundamental questions about the origin and the end of life).

The first articles she wrote on Buddhism, between 1893 and 1901, prefigure the new orientation she wanted to give Buddhism, that of a philosophical, social and political project entirely dedicated to the eradication of human suffering and the establishment of "universal fraternity." This project is based on a materialist worldview, which is described as intellectually superior, since it comes from the great Aryan civilization, and not from a bunch of neurotic Galilean fishermen. Indeed, her apology for Buddhism is inseparable from this denigration of Christianity, which is presented not in any serious theological or historical framework, but as the despicable caricature proliferated in many Parisian intellectual circles.

At this stage of her training in Buddhism, Louise David had accumulated knowledge from various sources and had made drastic personal choices. First, she rejected the common understanding of esotericism and distanced herself from other Theosophists who supported a materialistic conception of religion. This deconstruction of esotericism is twofold. On the one hand, the "highest teachings of the Buddha," reserved for the intellectual elite of humanity, is not secret but is a rationalist philosophy very few people can understand. On the other hand, she identifies the complex doctrines and rituals often described as occult or esoteric by her contemporaries as purely products of the physical environment.

She confirmed this ambientist theory in two articles published in 1900 and 1901, entitled *De l'importance des influences ambiantes au point de vue philosophique* (About the Importance of Ambiant Influences on Philosophy) and *De l'origine physique des mythes et de leur influence sur les institutions sociales* (On the Physical Origins of Myths and Their Influence on Social Institutions).[99] Then she developed a radically anti-Christian, and more generally anti-spiritualist, conception of Buddhism. The latter was assimilated into a kind of socialist doctrine, with notions such as universal happiness and universal fraternity favored over ideas of otherworldly salvation. In the 1890s she also had the experience of contemplating Buddhist objects and witnessing Buddhist rituals, not only at the Guimet Museum but also during a journey to Ceylon, India, Indochina and Southern China, as an opera singer, between 1893 and 1896. It seems that she was not favourably impressed by the Annamite (Vietnamese) Buddhists she saw practicing their religion.

In an unpublished text probably written in the late 1890s about a trip to Indochina in 1896, titled *Notes sur le bouddhisme au Tonkin* (Notes on Buddhism in Tonkin), she writes: "Imagine a man who studied Buddhist literature, completely penetrated by the spirit of texts written at the original time of Buddhism. Imagine that he lands in Tonkin without being warned that the majority of the inhabitants of this country are classified as Buddhists.

He would never suspect, at first glance, that the religion of this people is Buddhism. What a vague word. What a throng of superstitions, of rites, of practices have been put under the name of 'Buddhist religion.' Probably because the Buddha's philosophy in no way lends itself to the construction of a religion, all the elements capable of constituting the religious edifice were borrowed from elsewhere, and when the edifice was erected, it was crowned with the Buddha's name."[100] She goes on to describe the various rites and beliefs she found there and explains that the Annamites themselves do not even pretend to be Buddhists. This confrontation between her intellectual, European conception of Buddhism and Asian religious practices would prefigure her experience in Sikkim several years later.

The Buddha's Real Teachings

Alexandra David's redefinition of Buddhism in modernist terms reached its climax in the years 1909-1911. In 1909, she published an article entitled *Quelques écrivains bouddhistes contemporains* (A few contemporary Buddhist writers)[101] in which she writes that, contrary to what most European scholars thought, Buddhism is not a fossil doctrine, but a living one. To know what the original doctrine of the Buddha really was, one needs to consider what a few contemporary Buddhist activists had to say. Of course, those modern Buddhists belong to the intellectual elite of their countries, they are not Ministers, nor members of traditional religious schools, which, as we have seen, are but corrupt superstitions.

She writes that, under the influence of the Western mind – that is to say, rationalism – many "ancient Indian doctrines," including Vedanta and Buddhism, are undergoing radical change. This change is not a betrayal of the original doctrines, as she noticed in Tonkin and other Asian countries, but on the contrary a return to the founders' actual thinking. David-Néel, in those years, clearly joined the modernist Buddhist movement – authentic Buddhism is the Buddha's original teachings, it is devoid of any supernatural or ritual dimensions and should be revived today.[102]

The writers she cites in this article – Anagarika Dharmapala, the director of the Maha Bodhi Society in Calcutta, Ananda Metteya, "an English writer among the already numerous groups of Western bikkhus," Maung Nee, described as "a Burmese" although he actually was an English convert also known as Bhikkhu Silacara, and P. Lakshmi Narasu, a "Hindu writer who studied in English universities" – are considered providential reformers.

She writes that most Asian people did not understand Buddhism and that Western intellectuals or Asian thinkers with a Western background were needed to remind them of what the Buddha actually taught: "The Orient has very badly used the high notions that the Buddha tried to disseminate there. The least degenerate sects we find there are very distant from his mind, and, without doubt, it is from our thought, if not from our blood, that the new Luther, necessary to Buddhist reformation, will come."[103]

It is therefore the role of enlightened Westerners like herself to bring back true Buddhism to Asia and to the world. It is from this viewpoint, which she may have borrowed from de Rosny, that David-Néel's early career in the East should be understood.

The article describes the thought and works of those Buddhist activists and how they could be useful in the project of regenerating both the West and the Orient. About Anagarika Dharmapala, the Sinhalese Buddhist revivalist who took an active part in the 1893 Parliament of the World's Religions in Chicago, she says that he described "the Buddhist attitude" in such a way that any comparison with Christianity was impossible. Buddhism prescribes the use of reason and reveals that "injustice, fear, hatred, and ignorance are the vices that oppose human progress" and that the truth of impermanence dissolves all metaphysical questions into mere absurdity.[104]

Ananda Metteya, the British convert whose life shows that "Buddhism includes no dogma nor pontiff," "no vow of obedience," is described as "the founder of the International Buddhist Society" established in Burma. He might be considered a monk – since Western vocabulary, so infused with Christian references, does not provide another word – but only if one "considers monastic life only as a convenient way to study, meditate, or propagandize." She does not provide Ananda Metteya's real name, Charles Bennett, nor does she mention the fact that he once was a member of the Hermetic Order of the Golden Dawn, was an occultist and a close associate of the black magician Aleister Crowley.

The third author she mentions is Maung Nee, whose real (unmentioned) name was John Frederick S. McKechnie, a former English factory worker who became interested in Buddhism through the publications of Charles Bennett. He became a member of the International Buddhist Society in Burma and a novice in 1906 under Nyanatiloka, a German convert.

Alexandra David does not offer any information on the backgrounds of her modernist heroes, although she was probably aware of their personal stories, since she regularly met English Buddhists and Theosophists in London between 1906 and 1911. It is, in fact, through her British Theosophical connections that she discovered these modernist authors – none other than the intellectual mahatmas she was searching for. David-Néel's unpublished correspondence mentions that she stayed at least twice in England for an extended period, once in 1906 when she stayed at her friend's Marguerite's place in Ealing and visited the British Library, and in August 1910 when she attended meetings and spoke at conferences at the London Buddhist Society.[105]

In this article she informs her readers about the book recently published by Maung Nee, *Lotus Blossoms* (1907). She describes it as "a kind of manual, offering in a very succinct format a very clear idea of Buddhism freed from all heterogeneous superstitions."

She lavishes praise on it – the book is "well organized, clear, and erudite." Maung Nee insists on impermanence and the illusion of the self, "gives advice on careful agnosticism," and insists on the "human and natural nature of Buddhism." Maung Nee's teachings also include a particular approach to morality, which "has no intrinsic value," contrary to what is taught in Christian countries, but is only "an excellent way, a necessary hygiene for those pursuing wisdom."[106] Passions, which lead to what is commonly called "immorality," make the mind unclear, and an unclear mind does not reflect reality faithfully. To keep one's own mind as pure as still water, it is therefore necessary to avoid passions and their fruit, immoral behaviour – but in themselves, crimes and sins are in no way blameworthy.

The last author she cites is Professor P. Lakshmi Narasu, from Madras. She states that he was educated in English universities (whether it was in Britain or in India is not mentioned) and has "degrees in sciences, rather than in letters." However, she writes, Narasu can read several languages, including Latin, Greek, German and French. He has "read all our philosophers from the most ancient to the latest." In his book, *The Essence of Buddhism* (1907), Narasu, like David-Néel, considers property "a social problem" and declares that Buddhism is nothing other than socialism: "The spirit of Buddhism is essentially socialist, that is to say it teaches the union of combined actions for a social purpose. It is totally opposed to this industrialism with its fight without remission, without scruples, and without pity for riches, considered the object of the supreme human efforts, which gnaws at the so-called developed nations…" He goes on to explain that capital is not the product of savings but of theft, that workers are exploited "for the comfort and pleasure of a few," and that Buddhism condemns theft in all its forms.[107]

David-Néel is also impressed by the way Narasu is tolerant towards people who think they are practicing Buddhism but are simply behaving superstitiously: "Considering his Oriental coreligionists and the miserable superstitions in which they indulge, he suppresses the revolt that rises in his mind at the sight of those ridiculous practices with which the name of the ardent apostle of reason and intelligence is associated. For those who childishly bathe a Buddha statue in scented water and put garlands of flowers around it, he only has a compassionate thought of pity."

Furthermore, Narasu writes that "the highest truths exceed the intellectual capacity of vulgar minds, whereas the ablutions of sacred images can be practiced by all," and one should not condemn the vulgar minds for their inferiority, since they are not even aware of it. "The conclusion is simple," David-Néel writes, paraphrasing Narasu: "The Buddhist with a developed mind will show no malicious contempt for the simple ones who mesmerize themselves with childish practices." She then quotes a long excerpt from a chapter of *The Essence of Buddhism* entitled "Death and After," to show how different Buddhist and Christian funerals are. It is not surprising that David-Néel attributes the last and longest part of her article to Narasu. Indeed, he seems to sum up the idea she formulated in this period: Buddhism is another, Indian name for socialism.

Her 1911 book on Buddhism, entitled *Le modernisme bouddhiste ou le bouddhisme du Bouddha* (Buddhist Modernism or the Buddha's Buddhism),[108] deals with the development of these ideas. As the title indicates, she understands the Buddha's original doctrine as inherently modern, i.e., philosophically materialist and politically socialist. Conversely, the teachings of her socialist mahatmas are presented as authentically Buddhist. This is the thesis of the book. *Le modernisme bouddhiste* is essentially based on the writings of Maung Nee, Narasu, and Dharmapala and a few books by Sorbonne professors such as Sylvain Lévi and other European scholars such as Thomas and Caroline Rhys Davids, Max Müller and Hermann Oldenberg. The book quotes from modernist authors and from the Sanskrit texts they use. *Le modernisme bouddhiste* has seven chapters: The Buddha, The Four Noble Truths, Meditation, Karma, Nirvana, Sangha, and Two Contemporary Problems in Modernist Buddhism.

The Buddha is presented as "literally, the one who knows,"[109] "a historical figure,"[110] and a social reformer: "if not a revolutionary, at least the leader of social causes."[111] Her chapter on the Four Noble Truths is a development of what she had already written in previous articles about suffering (its unacceptability, the possibility and necessity of destroying it completely, with Bodhi, Knowledge or Intelligence as the way to do so). The book also reflects the academic knowledge of her day with many quotes from the *Dhammapada* and various sutras. The chapter on meditation does not describe any ritual practices, dismissed as late inventions by superstitious Asians, but consists in enthusiastic praise for both the intellect and "the Hindu."[112]

She describes a Buddhist equivalent of the Christian examination of consciousness[113] and another purely intellectual practice, which consists in trying to "establish firmly within oneself good tendencies of the mind," based on the *Mahā-sudassan-sutta*.[114] She also explains that the Buddhists practice the "contemplation of the body," which includes the contemplation of cadavers, sensations and thoughts in order to realize the impermanence of the self.[115] She then talks about *Samma-Samādhi*, or Right Concentration, and says this meditation has nothing to do with what people in the West think about it: it is not, she writes, "the Buddhist opium" or the "Buddhist torpor" many Europeans imagined it was. It is only a way to focus one's mind. There is nothing mystical about it. She describes the different kinds of effort necessary to reach a perfectly peaceful and detached state of mind.

Her chapter on Karma explains the Hindu origins of the notion. She says that the Buddha did not add any innovation to this concept.[116] She insists, on the other hand, on the differences between karma and Christian notions of eternal soul and uses Nietzschean terminology to explain how karma surpasses the Western understanding of morality. Karma, she writes, is beyond good and evil and exposes the moral and cultural relativism she mentioned in previous articles.[117] She then explains how the notion of nirvana has been wrongly understood in the West.[118] She writes that the importance of this notion has been exaggerated, since the most ancient Buddhist texts do not talk about nirvana, but about "the Arahat state," "the highest degree of holiness-wisdom." She describes it as "a mental state realised on this earth by a living being (the Arahat) and not a Paradise only reachable after death." She states that the Buddha's original doctrine never mentions ideas of rewards after death. To her, Buddhism is an immanent doctrine, and its practices, exclusively intellectual, lead to complete liberation from all physical and social determinants (Knowledge), which is "wisdom."[119]

In her chapter on the sangha, she explains that, based on Hendrik Kern's *Histoire du bouddhisme dans l'Inde*,[120] religious communities had always existed in India and were not a Buddhist invention. The role of those communities was to help individuals renounce the world and study. She writes: "The Buddhist bikshu [sic] is a copy, almost identical, of his Brahmanist predecessor."[121] He is a person whose intellectual level is beyond the norm and who wishes to dedicate his life to the pursuit of wisdom. The chapter shows what counted for Alexandra David in traditional Indian forms of religious life (study, reflection, knowledge, detachment from the world) and why she decided to visit India to meet Aryas. In her mind, these were living doubles of the historical Buddha. In her last chapter, "Two Contemporary Problems in Modernist Buddhism,"[122] she discusses the necessary changes to the status of women in Buddhism that activists should champion and the solutions to "the social question" that Buddhist intellectuals should seek.[123]

Louise David's conception of Buddhism can be interpreted as a cultural translation, based on her rejection of the traditional Catholic worldview that was still dominant, though endangered, in the late 19th and early 20th centuries in France. She arrived at this translation in two stages.

First came a re-writing of the Christian worldview in materialist and socialist language, with all the modifications it entails. Certain traditional notions remain but have their names changed and their meaning slightly modified. "Charity" becomes "solidarity" and should be provided not by members of the Church but by members of "Society" or "the State" (the new and only legitimate earthly communities). "Fraternity" remains fraternity but no longer finds any legitimacy in the idea of a Heavenly Father (it is not explained why all men are brothers; it is simply a new article of faith). The equality of all men before God, again traditionally explained by the notion of a divine father who loves his children equally, is divested of any justification (it is therefore "irrational") and should become manifest in all human life's dimensions, thanks to the active intervention of the State (a new messiah). "Freedom" replaces "free will" and no longer consists in the individual's capacity to judge and act independently of the conditions of his life, but on his "right" (a notion that replaces "duty") to act as he wishes, independently of common morality, decency or habits.

There can be no free will, according to many socialists and sociologists of the time, since all human behavior, thoughts, feelings and values (i.e., human culture) are only the products of their environment. Indeed, certain traditional notions are not just transformed and renamed, they are completely dismissed. This is the case with free will and with all things pertaining to the spiritual and supernatural realms: the notions of spirit, God, afterlife, paradise, etc. Only the material aspects of life count, and a real paradise should be built on earth independently of (or in opposition to) any Biblical revelation – from which, nonetheless, all the elements of those new materialist soteriologies are borrowed.

We saw how common this type of enterprise was in 19th-century occultist and socialist circles. From among all the diverse anti-Christian – even heretic – reform movements surrounding her, Alexandra David's choice is far from original. She adopted the views of the school that was becoming dominant, notably within the French government of her time but also in many socialist parties in Europe - and which would soon give birth to unprecedented totalitarian revolutions worldwide.

Her innovation was to adopt, systematize and popularize the modernist conceptions of a few Buddhist political activists who had already proceeded to a second translation – from a socialist worldview to a Buddhist one. "Fraternity" becomes "interdependence," physical and social "determinism" becomes "karma," the perfect knowledge of determinisms that liberates the individual becomes "nirvana."

Although she cites many traditional sources and assimilates the academic knowledge of the most erudite European scholars, her description of Buddhism remains a hybrid doctrine typical of late 19th and early 20th century ideologies – halfway between a religious movement and a political program.[124] It is founded on a sharp critique of Christianity and of the culture it produced, while still being entirely based on the worldview, stories and values of the traditional Western world. It is in this sense that she is modern.

As the French philosopher and historian Rémi Brague has noted,[125] the most characteristic trait of modernity is probably the attitude of "parasitizing" the European medieval heritage, which drew cultural content from two external sources: Greco-Roman antiquity and the Judeo-Christian Biblical tradition. Modern thinkers, Brague says, are prisoners of medieval conceptions of the world, while pretending to reject and replace them with other ideas. In fact, they do not really borrow ideas from elsewhere (as medieval thinkers did), they only exhaust the rich European cultural well from which their seemingly new ideas materialize.

Alexandra David conceived of Buddhism in materialist and socialist terms, without knowing that her revolutionary ideas were themselves deeply rooted in ancient Christian beliefs. She was, then, a rather conventional modernist.

4

Daughter of the French Enlightenment

Man is definitely a wicked beast.

Alexandra David-Néel
Correspondance avec son mari, 1918

The Victory of Materialism over Spiritualism

The usual categorizing of Alexandra David-Néel as a master of spirituality inclines the reader to think that, if she were a free thinker at all, she most likely belonged to the spiritualist, rather than the materialist, category. It is, in any case, what her previous biographers implicitly suggest or confidently write.[127]

However, her first published text (1900), which exposes her vision of humanity, does not confirm the hypothesis. *Pour la Vie*[128] (a short book she was able to publish through her father's connections, despite being an uneducated young woman) aims at "explaining all social facts." It identifies what human life should naturally be, what it accidentally is, and why and how it should be regenerated.

The text starts with a definition of man, whom she calls "an organism." Its main feature is to strive to live – hence the manifesto's title – in a threatening environment. Life itself is defined, in a very materialistic way, as a constant effort to meet one's own primary needs: to get food and protect one's own physical integrity. As she writes, "Eating, everything revolves around that."[129] Man is thus no different from any other animal, as he needs to compete for survival. He is subject to the Darwinian law of natural selection: "As soon as an organism is formed, all its forces tend towards a single goal: maintaining its personal existence by giving it food and defending it against any influence that may destroy or diminish it."[130]

The organism has no conscience. The human being is only composed of matter, coming from the food he eats daily. Thinking and the "illusion of conscience" merely emerge from the brain, genetically influenced by one's parents. The shape of our ancestors' brains determines what we think, in the exact same way physical characteristics such as the shape of a nose or the colour of a beard are transmitted from one generation to the next.[131]

From that materialistic tenet, Louise David (under the pen name of Alexandra Myrial), envisioning a shift from Christianity to Socialism,[132] logically infers two important ideas: first, that there is no free will, since every thought and action is determined by heredity, and second, that change from one generation to the next can only occur by a change of circumstances.[133] Circumstances can actually change the way the brain functions (i.e., how the brain *adapts* to its new environment in pursuit of its sole aim of survival). The reverse is also true; the brain, and therefore thought, is also influenced by the organism and the food it eats. One's digestion, metabolism, body temperature, wellbeing or stress, health or disease, all directly impact the way one thinks. The connection between body and cognition is made by the sensations, which produce information in the brain, coming from the body.[134]

Another consequence of this biological conception of the human being is that the individual cannot be held accountable for his actions. Since there is no free will, but mere adaptation to the environment, there cannot be any personal responsibility, nor any form of morality. Everyone should do as they please: "No one is responsible, science says, since no one is free to determine at their pleasure the exterior causes under the which they act; since no one is free to choose the elements that constitute their organism... By declaring human will subject to causes that determined its manifestation, science reveals the old saying: *Do as you like*."[135]

The individual should therefore not feel guilty about, or even responsible for wanting, the things he thinks he needs. Rules and laws that tell him those desires are either forbidden or sinful cannot be legitimate, since they do not correspond to the normal, natural human condition – which is to be selfish. Apart from personal interest, she writes, there is "no other secret in the universe; each individuality behaves according to *what it is*."

There is "no trace of government in the universe, so why imagine that man should be an exception?" Life is nothing but "the incessant movement of molecular individualities coming together according to their composition and to the milieus in which they meet." What man should look for, she writes, is "happiness of all through the happiness of each one."[136] All forms of human rules (morals, religion, laws, justice, property), in all societies are just "fictitious personalities" invented and imposed by powerful people and institutions to exert authority over others and appropriate more resources.

In the first stages of humanity, the powerful invented gods to justify their authority and superiority. In later stages, the gods were replaced by other fictitious notions, such as "conscience," which gave birth to "so-called secular morals" and other laws. The root cause of the denaturation of man, which led him to abandon the concern for his own welfare, is "the fatal influence of abstract authorities: the ideas, religious and other types of myths, customs, etc. All those external manifestations of authority still have their source in a mental authority. No material authority, that of laws, or that of the individuals, bears its own force and its own reason in itself. None of them is actually exerted by itself, all of them are based on ideas. And it is because man bows first of all before those ideas that he comes to accept their tangible realisation in the various forms taken by the authority principle."[137]

These abstract authorities, the most powerful of which is religion, came to replace physical strength in man's effort to dominate his fellow man. Alexandra Myrial explains that there are two phases in the construction of religious and political authority. First, in a "nearly animal state," the weakest obeys the strongest "because he cannot do otherwise" – it is the realm of pure physical strength. Then the weakest continues to obey "because he thinks he must obey." The strongest has successfully managed to instil in the weakest a series of rational justifications for his domination. Among all these abstract ideas invented to enslave other people, it is the moral and religious ideas that rank first. Instead of forcing a neighbour to obey by saying "I want you to do this," the perverse ruling class uses the symbolic power of religious institutions to say, "you must bow."[138]

According to the young Alexandra Myrial, even modern societies, supposedly characterized by secularization, are still based on illegitimate, manipulative and illusory concepts derived from religion.[139] The proof of religion's pernicious resistance is found in the falsely secularized notion of conscience. "The gods can disappear, humanity has replaced them; for their own enslavement, they invented a secularized god, an intimate tyranny: conscience." Conscience doesn't exist, since its material proof cannot be given: "…conscience, of which no anatomist ever found the organ under his scalpel."[140]

These abstract ideas not only control human beings' minds with artificial notions of good and evil, but they also give birth to a profusion of "fictitious personalities," fake identities and feelings that humans create in order to comply with what the strongest in society expect. The individual loses touch with his own needs and desires and becomes a slave to the many "spooks" of himself that he created.[141] Contrary to the Christian moral code under which she was raised, egoistic desires do not have to be suppressed or controlled. They should be considered as they are: a driving force leading to one's happiness.

In France, the major source of oppression is, of course, the Roman Catholic Church, not only because of its self-sacrificing and demanding morality, but because it also believes in free will, a falsely generous idea that allows for notions of culpability, justice, law, control of the mind, repression and punishment. It also keeps men in a mental prison through the use of theatrical performances and unrealistic promises of solace: "Christianity, by persuading men to take pride in alleged freedom, only contributed to add another form of enslavement, which nothing justifies, of the individual to the rest of society. That false notion of freedom has never been anything but a trap designed to deprive man of his real freedom, the freedom to pursue his desires."[142] To avoid such enslavement, the individuals should "first of all convince themselves of the non-existence of all fictitious personalities."[143]

They should also learn to "seek happiness in the present," in other words, to satisfy their immediate needs and yearnings, although it may be difficult after centuries of oppression by so-called education or, more correctly, false and perverse indoctrination.[144] This should be replaced by "true education," that is to say a new habit to take that consists in listening to one's own deepest desires.[145] One should learn that selfishness is not reprehensible – it is, on the contrary, the root cause and only condition of happiness: "If, finding selfish and restricted the conception of individual, immediate, entirely self-centred happiness, one prefers, by a residue of attachment to wrong ideas of the past, to give oneself the distant goal of humanity's future happiness, one still needs to recognize the necessity to work for one's own well-being."[146]

To find true and lasting happiness, the organism must restore its natural freedom – not the freedom to choose its actions according to some transcendent principle, but a license to satisfy basic desires. Man should "destroy all prejudices within himself, all the hindrances which oppose his freedom of action" and "strive, in all things including the smallest, to always have his true happiness in sight."[147] The destruction of prejudices and the happiness that supposedly naturally derives from it will happen through the systematic use of science: "[suffering] will exist as long as man will seek his rule of conduct outside science."[148] "It is to science and experience alone that man must ask for his rule of conduct and the direction he should take in life." "Science, free search, make living and active men; obedience makes dead."[149] "Only knowledge and experience are capable of indicating to man what suits his nature."[150] "Isn't science the greatest guardian of human life, isn't it she who teaches us what disease is, who teaches us to defeat with hygiene the morbid influences that may attack our organisms, to bring them disorder and even kill them?"[151] "Humanity, enlightened by the teachings of science… should also strive to destroy the causes of harmful actions and organize mental hygiene."[152] "Science will kill old-fashioned morals."[153] It is not clear, however, what science exactly is – besides the medical sphere, understood as the positive knowledge of the human body and all the techniques related to its treatment, and the antichristian context where science opposes superstition.

Louise David, aka Alexandra Myrial, wrote those words around 1898 at the age of thirty and seems to have subscribed to them until her death.[154] They express her conception of humanity, which contains nothing spiritual. She depicts man as a mere biological organism with no conscience, whose sole aim is to fulfil its needs for food to survive in a competitive environment where only the strong succeed.

Man is conceived as individual, as opposed to social, and his fellow humans seem to exist only to impose domination and authority over him. Man's original sin – so to speak – is his weakness for believing in the abstract ideas invented by others to undermine him. The key to his happiness is to realise these are merely productions, illusions of the mind devoid of any concrete reality and thus of any legitimacy, which he must not allow to control him. Man should return to his natural state, where the individual's free will is the only rule to follow.

However, his will is portrayed as passive rather than active, it is not a positive choice but a basic recognition of the various tendencies and "influences" that guide him in certain directions in life. Man cannot choose to think and behave in one way or another, because he has no free will – a false Christian notion invented to control people from the inside of their fake conscience without resorting to physical violence. Having no free will, he cannot be held responsible for his actions, which in turn implies that there should be no laws or morals, all instruments of domination.

According to Louise David's thinking, the awakened man needs only the lucidity and the courage to acknowledge he is not free but, rather, a passive object in the hands of Nature. As a natural element, man is entirely biological. His mind is the product of his brain, mostly the result of heredity and food, and secondarily the manifestation of his historical and cultural environment. The process of thinking is purely organic. It comes from the sensations and is constructed in the brain through experience. There are no innate ideas or natural predispositions (except the need to eat and survive); everything is acquired from the environment through the five senses. Only science, understood in the medical sense, can fully explain the individual (that is to say, his mechanisms, a very 18th-century term) and provide him with a rule of life, mostly physical hygiene. "Mental hygiene" is also mentioned as a necessary public policy, without further explanation. One can deduce that some form of re-education is required to teach individuals how to get rid of their fictitious personalities and understand what they truly are: just one species of animal.

This worldview is typical of the scientific discourse on salvation that emerged in the 19th century and gave rise, despite their supposedly objective and neutral stance, to various ideological, religious, and political enterprises seeking to create "a new man." We see this in Auguste Comte's positivism, Emile Durkheim's sociology, and in Socialism, Marxism, Leninism, Fascism, etc. That such revolutionary doctrines emerged from champions of the French Republic and adherents of Free Thought, usually credited with a charitable vision of mankind, is not surprising in the light of recent historiographical scholarship. Indeed, the French historian Xavier Martin has shown that the conception of the human being promoted by French revolutionaries and, before them, French Enlightenment philosophers, is in fact pessimistic, materialistic, utilitarian and sensualist. Man is reduced to either an animal or a machine, unable to think, condemned only to react to sensations triggered by a single motive – selfishness.[155]

For Enlightenment thinkers, how Christianity explained the existence of a human soul, independent of matter and free to choose between good and evil, is considered superstition and prejudice. There is no active principle in man – except perhaps in a few members of the self-proclaimed elite, the philosophers themselves.[156] Subjected to his basic needs and passions, man is incapable of any true act of generosity or compassion. Such virtues, as well as laws and morals, are just hypocritical inventions that enable man to have a good opinion of himself. Reason, according to the revolutionary thinkers that inspired David-Néel, really means instrumental reason, economical reason – in other words, selfishness.

These beliefs, which surprisingly escaped the attention of previous biographers, are in sharp contrast to other early writings, notably her personal diaries, in which she implores God to help her find her way in life.[157] Her private notebooks, discovered after her death by her last secretary, Marie-Madeleine

Peyronnet, show a dramatic evolution between 1889 and 1892 (about a decade before she published *Pour la Vie*), with the young Louise David losing her faith in the Christian God. They start with lyrical praise to God, who "saved [her] from idolatry and made [her] understand and admire the sublime harmony of the heavens," and finish with the dramatic confession of her disbelief, for which she still asks for God's mercy.

She gives the impression of trying hard to believe in God's existence but being tragically unable to do so. At the very end of the notebooks, she writes derisively of the Christian belief in the Ascension, sealing her definitive rejection of Christianity. It is not clear, however, whether she became an atheist immediately after she renounced her parents' faith or if she first tried to find other more satisfactory conceptions of God before reaching that materialistic conclusion. It is highly probable that she explored many alternative religions in the sincere hope of finding Truth before becoming dissatisfied with them all and joining the ranks of the growing atheist camp.

The notebooks already give many clues about such religious longings, which she later denied and described with caustic irony.[158] These include her identification as an "MTS" (most probably a Member of the Theosophical Society), her references to the Zodiac, the Koran (which she says she read), Plato, the Rig Vedas, the Hindu god Agni, the Hebraic name for God, Adonai, which all tend to confirm that she was seriously interested in esoteric knowledge.

Apostasy: a French Literary and Political Fashion

It is clear from her notebooks that during her twenties Louise David lost her faith in God, relinquished her religious vocation, and adopted a markedly critical view of Christianity. The evolution can be explained on a psychological level by her pride and her acknowledged inability to renounce worldly ambitions. She also wrote much later, in a posthumous volume,[159] that she expected to find mystery in religion, as well as an austere way of practicing it. Religion, in other words, had to introduce her to an extraordinary, awe-inspiring, otherworldly reality. It could not be accessible to simple people in their daily lives; it had to be divested of any kind of triviality.

This is how she explained her disillusionment with Catholicism: "My incursion behind the disturbing mystery of the gates and veils [of the Carmel order] left me very disillusioned. The other side of that shadowy boarder, seen from the chapel of the nuns, had nothing hallucinating anymore. It only showed very big, vulgar cotton sheets, identical to those that one hangs in cloakrooms to protect the clothes from dust and daylight. The Carmelites did not look like the idea I had conceived of them either, based on the virgins with hieratic attitudes that appeared to me on floors dotted with lilies and in old cathedrals' stained glass. My hostesses did not differ from my secular compatriots, good Flemings with pink cheeks, whose plump curves lifted the sackcloth scapular and who in their rustic garden, instead of lilies, grew cabbages."[160]

There was, then, a huge discrepancy between her dreams of spirituality and what religious institutions had to offer. Because reality did not conform to her ideals, both were illegitimate. She was not the type to find grandeur in the quotidian "small way," like her contemporary, the Carmelite Thérèse de Lisieux,[161] and she certainly did not taste the Sulpician religious sensitivity of the time.[162]

Louise David's evolution from the Christian faith to a materialistic worldview can also be explained by the intellectual and political context of her time. The ideology promoted by the Republicans (in which she was initiated by her father) evolved in the second half of the 19th century from anticlericalism to atheism.[163] It was not only a "practical atheism" (the wish to create a social and political life disconnected from religion, whatever the beliefs of private individuals), it also became a "theoretical atheism" with the very idea of

God severely attacked.[164] The German atheistic tradition, with the famous texts of Feuerbach, Marx and Nietzsche, is not mentioned in Louise David's notebooks. She seems to have become acquainted with atheism first through the works of French intellectuals, notably Ernest Renan and Jean Richepin, whom she cites in her notebooks. These authors exemplify the two different tendencies in French Free Thought. Renan was a deist writer and a specialist in Semitic languages who was one of the first to treat Jesus as a historical character deprived of any supernatural dimensions.[165] In contrast, the eccentric and unruly Richepin, a naturalist poet, novelist and dramatist, aimed at "taking atheism to its extremities," writing crude and provocative literature and actively promoting "blasphemies."[166]

The writing of blasphemies, as well as the "legal condemnation" and "public execution" of God (in effigy), illustrated the curious transition of Free Thought from the anticlerical tradition, which sought to build a society without any reference to God, to an active fight against something that was supposed not to exist.[167] We do not know whether Louise David wrote blasphemies (declarations of hatred toward a non-existent God) but she certainly was influenced by the writings of Richepin, which by their radicalism probably disinhibited the young woman's thoughts and propelled her on the exclusive path of the intellectually consistent few.

"I doubt that many people have the courage to follow, ring after ring, the logical string of my poems, to reach the implacable conclusion to which they necessarily lead," he wrote. "When I review the various opinions that I attack without any pity, opinions that often contradict one another but are all united against me, I wonder with anxiety whom my sincerity shall not hurt. Before anything else, I will scandalize the devotees, the faithful of organized religions, whichever they may be, and, in their eyes, I will commit nothing less than a sacrilege by disembowelling their idols to expose their inanity. Behind them, all the Deists will rebel, more or less disguised, *religioish* as others are religious, the worshippers of a Supreme Being, of a universal Conscience, of whatever Great-All, from the freethinkers who cling to the *trimurti* of the True, the Beautiful, and the Good, until the Pantheists who, by blowing into the impersonal God balloon, make it burst ad infinitum. In spite of their tolerance, the sceptics will be angry at my audacious claims… The materialists themselves, or at least those who proclaim themselves to be such and who are inconsistent enough to speak about causes and laws, will find me criminal and dangerous, to replace those causes by chance and those laws by habits. Men of science will never consent to despise the formulas of the discoveries that make their glory… The good people without any philosophical pretensions, who nonetheless imperially strut in their quality of men and who offer themselves the incense burner, under the pretext of adoring Reason, those amiable adorers of themselves, will bleed at the blows I thump to human smugness, and they will rebel to see me spit in their stupid incense burner."[168]

Richepin was not a philosopher but a poet, and Louise David seems to have enjoyed his extremism, though she could not find any positive philosophy in his works. She had to draw inspiration from other thinkers to arrive at the worldview revealed in *Pour la Vie*.

It was in anarchist circles, under the influence of the French geographer, writer and political activist Élisée Reclus (1830-1905), that she probably discovered other materialist and atheist thinkers. Reclus was one of the most famous libertarian thinkers of her time, an exiled Communard, the son of a Protestant minister, a Theology student who became a positivist and materialist, and a freemason, vegetarian and feminist, and the initiator of the Anti-Marriage movement. He was also a great traveller who wrote some of the first tourist guides before becoming a "social geographer." Reclus considered that human cultures were deeply influenced by their environment, even on a spiritual level, and thought that governments should not interfere with local ecosystems.[169] For him, man is part of nature before being part of society (even less of a creation), and society, like nature, should be free from any kind of government.

Louise David probably met him in the early 1890s in Brussels, where Reclus and his brother Élie, a journalist, writer, ethnologist, anarchist and freemason, were working on the foundation of a new free University to replace the *Université libre de Bruxelles*, which had dismissed Élisée from his post as a geographer in the Science Faculty. The connection might have been made through her close friend, the musician and political activist Jean Hautstont, whom she met in Brussels in 1893 at an anarchist club called The Crocodile.[170] Hautstont was probably introduced to her by their common friend, the Belgian painter and anarchist Louis Thévenet, whose sister Cécile, a singer who also studied at the Brussels conservatory, might have been Louise David's friend.

Élisée Reclus had been suspected by the French police of links to the numerous anarchist terrorist attacks that took place in France in 1892 and 1893. Although French and Belgian public opinion was shocked by the assassinations and demanded justice, Elisée Reclus defended the murderers by distributing on the campus a pamphlet titled "Why are we Anarchists." In it he condemned the bourgeoisie, the priests, kings, soldiers and judges, whom he accused of impoverishing the poor, who are then predestined to act violently. The overthrow of the State and of all kinds of authority, he added, is necessary, and he called for "all free men to act spontaneously," ostensibly justifying terror.[171] Outraged by the rector's decision to cancel his appointment, which for him was an unbearable restraint on his freedom of thought, Reclus, his brother and their freemason friends founded the *Université Nouvelle* (The New University). Launched in the headquarters of their lodge, *les Amis philanthropes* (The Philanthropist Friends), the institution promoted the works of positivists and materialists, functioning from 1894 to 1919.

There is no certainty that Louise David frequented this new atheistic university – though it is highly likely – but we know she gave a conference on Buddhism at the *Université libre* around the same period.[172] In any case, it is Reclus who launched her career as a political writer and journalist, as the foreword to *Pour la Vie* testifies. The geographer's influence on David-Néel clearly appears in her anarchist creed, her conversion to theoretical atheism, her passion for travel and ethnography, her feminism, her initial rejection of marriage, and in her (temporary) vegetarianism.

Through Reclus, Louise David was introduced to libertarian thinkers like Proudhon, Bakunin, Kropotkin and Stirner. She felt a special empathy with Stirner, who developed a nihilistic and provocative philosophy often referred to as "individualist anarchism" or "rational egoism." It is important to understand the basics of that philosophy, for it provides a key to both David-Néel's anarchist manifesto and the parallel emergence of her interest in Buddhism. According to Max Stirner (1806-1856),[173] the reality of the self is impossible to fully comprehend: it is both a vacuum and a creative capacity. As there can be no speculation about the self and its relation to either the material or the spiritual worlds, the self needs only be defined on a practical level. Stirner considers that one must follow what one's ego dictates and do anything to satisfy basic needs and desires. It would be irrational and destructive not to follow one's own interests. The world is just a "union of egoists," in which the only sacred entity is the individual's will. What people call religion or the sacred, the State, Society, the law, right, or morality are nothing but abstractions elaborated by the strongest in society to impose their will on others.

The voluntary egoist – as opposed to the involuntary egoist who tries to avoid becoming an egoist but consequently supports a deluded self-image of morality – should know these abstractions are not only illegitimate but in fact unreal, pure illusions or "spooks" in the mind. Each person should therefore define their own ego, be their own creature, complying with no absolute norm, whether religious, moral or cultural. There ought to be no rule dictating what one's own personality should be. The intelligent person should strive for release from the ties imposed by others and let free will prevail over all external determinants.

The reader can recognize the exact words Louise David used in *Pour la Vie*. Anticipating her subsequent passion for Buddhism, we see her thought developing on the notion of individual desires prevailing in society, on the reduction of all kinds of ideas to "illusions of the mind," on the quest for a remedy to personal suffering, and a focus on the problematic conception of the ego.

At this stage of her formation, Louise David was no longer the spiritual seeker her devotees claim she has always been. She had once been a sincere Christian, wanted to become a nun at some point, but under the influence first of her father's friends, then from her own research, she had become a strong proponent of materialism and rational egoism.

Establishing The Reign of Rational Women

It is in the same social networks that Louise David met with feminist activists such as Maria Deraismes (1828-1894), a feminist and anticlerical orator, rich bourgeois and lesbian, and Marguerite Durand (1864-1936), a former actress and founder of one of the first feminist newspapers, *La Fronde* (1897-1903).

Alexandra David became very interested in the feminist cause and started writing articles, notably in *La Fronde*, and participating in national and international feminist conferences such as the *Conseil national des femmes françaises* (National Council of French Women), a federation created in 1901 as a regional branch of the *International Council of Women* founded in the United States in 1888. She also participated in the Italian feminist federation and reported on their activities but was quite critical of the feminist *bourgeoises* she met there, who in her opinion were too economically privileged to legitimately defend women's rights.

Alexandra David believed the first right women should claim was not the right to vote but the right to be economically free, so as not to depend on any man. She agreed with the idea that men had enslaved women in almost every culture and that the time had come for them to "liberate from the patriarchy," its instrumental "oppressive religions," and all the "fables" men had invented about women to keep them in servitude. The application of those anarchist, socialist and Marxist theories to women's liberation was not self-evident, since most political thinkers of the time and from the age of Enlightenment were profoundly misogynistic.[174] It is a tiny group of women activists[175] who, like Olympe de Gouges during the 1789 Revolution, reinterpreted Human Rights as being in fact Men's Rights and therefore deemed that new rights be granted to women so they could be equal to men.

Alexandra David became aware of this new rhetoric through the feminists she met in esoteric circles. She probably was educated in radical feminism by Maria Deraismes, who used freemason networks to disseminate her ideas on the Church's responsibility for the centuries-long oppression of women.[176] Maria Deraismes was the daughter of a Parisian merchant who professed Voltairian ideas. He allowed her to study a vast variety of topics, including the Bible, Christian theology, Oriental religions, Ancient Greek and Latin, and Enlightenment philosophy. She became a free thinker, publicly professing anticlerical, atheistic and feminist ideas as a journalist and orator. Financially independent thanks to her parents' fortune, she was able to spend her life as a political activist.[177]

In 1892, Maria Deraismes was initiated into the *Les Libres Penseurs* (The Freethinkers) freemason lodge in Le Pecq, near Versailles. Although women could always be initiated into Freemasonry through rites of adoption as the wives, daughters or sisters of initiated brothers, Freemasonry had remained a male-oriented society.[178] When *Les Libres Penseurs* initiated Deraismes as a sister rather than an adopted member, the *Grande Loge Symbolique Écossaise*, to which the lodge pledged allegiance as as affiliate, expelled them from the order, casting out Deraismes, her initiators and her brothers.

Resolved to be recognized as an authentic mason and to open masonic initiation to other women, she and a political activist, physician and senior mason, Dr Georges Martin, conceived of a new mixed masonic structure. In 1893 they initiated 15 female masons, among them Louise David and several other intellectuals and socialists. These included Clémence Royer (who translated Darwin's *The Origin of Species* into French); Eliska Vincent, socialist activist and cofounder of the *Société pour la revendication du droit des femmes* (Society for the Advocacy of Women's Rights); and Marie Béquet de Vienne, who created structures to help indigent pregnant women and promote breastfeeding. Politically committed to reforming society based on uncompromising republican ideas, the lodge has been thriving ever since, first becoming an international masonic order in 1901. Several members of the Theosophical Society became members of the order, including Annie Besant, George Arundale and Charles Leadbeater who introduced Freemasonry into India. Co-Freemasonry, as it was called in English, became intrinsically linked with Theosophy.[179]

In this lodge the young Louise-Alexandra David underwent rites of passage common to all varieties of Freemasonry, including the ceremony of the murder and resurrection of Hiram at the master's level and probably other rituals specific to the Human Right Order. Since most activities are secret, we do not know what grade Alexandra David reached in the masonic hierarchy. What we can reasonably deduce from the texts she published from the mid-1890s to the 1910s is that this radical feminist group had a profound influence on how she came to understand human relationships in general and relationships between men and women in particular. It is probably also within these circles that she defined exactly what she meant by "rational," the fundamental Enlightenment notion she applied first to feminism and then to Buddhism. Therefore, if we want a clearer understanding of her definition of Buddhism as a rational doctrine, it is useful to see what she meant by rational feminism – the title she gave to one of her more substantial feminist texts.[180]

Le féminisme rationnel (Rational Feminism) is one of the first texts in which she mentions Buddhism. Indeed, she starts with a Buddhist epigraph and praise for the Buddha, from whom, she says, she borrowed a "scientific" or "algebraic" method: the identification of women's suffering, its cause, and its solution. At this point in her intellectual life, it seems Buddhism interested her because it offered, in the form of the Four Truths for the Noble, a template of logical reasoning that could be applied to any kind of practical situation. The mention of Buddhism also set her apart from other feminists, in the way the mahatmas had made Blavatsky original among the legion of mediums of her time. Alexandra David starts her article with four long paragraphs (suffering, the cause of suffering, the cessation of suffering, and the path to the cessation of suffering) and then develops her ideas in a more conventional style, with no real connection to Buddhist doctrines.

Rather, in this and other articles, she adopts the stereotypical feminist writing style of the time, a lyrical, rich, elegant, but somehow repetitive and exaggerated language, the extensive use of dark and dramatic depictions of the feminine condition that is assumed to have remained unchanged for centuries. In *Vieilles rangaines*,[181] she states that women need to definitively break with their feminine ancestors, who all led a miserable life of "absolute annihilation." In preceding generations, she writes, "almost all women were either libertine or devout, often both at the same time, going from their lovers to their confessors, completely incapable of fully remaining themselves."[182] If one goes back in history, she adds, to the time of the Franks and the Gauls, one finds that "the male was dragging us after him, like the innumerable women we keep seeing today, bent under the weight of tents, households utensils, luggage of all kinds, following on foot behind the master who rides freely at the head of the caravan."[183] In a nutshell: "The whole of women's life has been there, for centuries: in that silent, degrading, and painful war (with men)."[184]

Women, however, quickly understood that they had some power over men and so took advantage of their beauty. Doing so, however, they became trapped in the vicious cycle of prostitution, portrayed as the lot of most – if not all – women: "Aren't women who deploy their grace, display their skilfully combined toilet, lavish smiles and amiability in order to get what they desire, taking a first step on the slope that imperceptibly leads to the courtesan – recognized as such, living exclusively from her beauty and the art of exciting men's desires? Is prostitution only represented by the miserable wandering on the pavement?"[185]

Prostitution is thus described by Alexandra David as the logical consequence of the feminine condition of her time. In 19th-century France the most valued role for a woman was motherhood. Women who did not marry and bear children were often considered failures. They would be spinsters worthy only of pity, or become nuns and gain quiet respectability, or try to make money out of their charms. That did not necessarily mean selling sex on the street or in houses of ill repute but concerned all the positions women could find in the theatre and the arts, either as actresses, singers, dancers or models.[186]

In late 19th-century Paris a few courtesans had a large and opulent clientele and became popular figures, sometimes venerated as semi-goddesses, as in the cases of Liane de Pougy, la Belle Otéro, la Païva, Marie Duplessis or Mata Hari. Such independent businesswomen, who gained wealth and social status through their disdain for social and moral conventions, their intrepidity, their elegance, wit and sexual skills, certainly occupied an ambiguous position in French society. The jealousy and contempt they aroused among other women, either the respectable bourgeois wives or the uncompromising rebels like Alexandra David, set them apart from society and condemned them to isolation. Although free and economically independent, the *demi-mondaines* could not become a feminist model, as their activity confined them to the sexual realm, which was, and still is, considered immoral.

The interesting suggestion that Alexandra David made is that their fate was not fundamentally different from that of respectable bourgeois mothers – a claim that must have scandalized French society. In Louise David's texts both are described as being compelled to become men's "baby dolls" and "women toys."[187] She reasoned that the way society functioned inevitably led women to prostitution. Women only had a right to choose between different kinds of prostitution, either as a real sex vendor on the street, as an actress or as a housewife. The only alternative was the religious life as a nun, but that, according to Alexandra David, was also a life of oppression, since the Church could never deliver anything but slavery. In this intellectual context, it is quite surprising that Louise David chose to become an opera singer.

Between the life of a prostitute and the life of an oppressed nun, a third approach was possible, which she called "rational feminism." To be a rational feminist, a woman who does not surrender her will and personal desires to another (either a man or God), one first needs to identify the cause of the problem, and then to suppress it. In an article titled *Question pressante* (Burning Question), she writes, "Many are the obstacles encountered by women, many are the reasons that keep her submitted… The most formidable, the one which is the initial cause of the evolution that through the centuries has forged this feminine type, so strangely different from the male type, the one to which, in my opinion, we should not surrender, is maternity."[188]

"Maternity," she wrote elsewhere and in many other instances, "is the obstacle."[189] "Incontestably," she writes, "maternity is the serious obstacle which opposes women's complete emancipation. It is the initial cause which, in the olden times of Prehistory, attached women to the cave."[190] Women who bear children are compared to weak animals, and there seems to be no place for joy, pleasure or sentiments in her description of maternity. Pregnancies (the cause of all evil) is described as "periods of absolute incapacity during which women are just good enough to drag themselves from deck chair to bed."[191]

"Maternity does not deserve the glory of apotheosis nor the shame of the Gemonians, it is a simple physiological function from which there is no pride nor humiliation to derive,"[192] she writes. Its glorification is a lie imputable to Christianity: "Christianity, a deathly religion which exalts absolute chastity and the annihilation of the senses, has nevertheless not tried to attack certain general feelings by proscribing 'the mother'. It admits her, at a very humble place, very far from the place it attributes to the virgins, but still it accepts her, it blesses her, even makes maternity the excuse for and the condition of the affection it condescends to show her."[193] Maternity is the cause of women's decline, the cause of their "enslavement."[194]

Although in all other parts of life, human beings should follow their natural desires and satisfy their most basic needs – as established in *Pour la Vie* – the rational woman, on the other hand, should not be reduced to her physiological dimensions and should avoid maternity at all costs, for maternity "enslaves her to the physiological level."[195] Physiology is thus a good thing in human beings in general, the only reality that counts, but a bad thing where reproduction is concerned. Nature and physiology are notions that Alexandra David uses contradictorily, and only in service of her own views about what intelligent women should be. They should not be a mother, a nun, or someone who pleases the opposite sex with her beauty and charm, but an independent and proud individual who dedicates her life to more intellectual activities. In other words, the rational woman is none other than herself. But she seemed to distrust the idea that some women might actually want to be wives, mothers, nuns or seductresses.

In fact, a note in one of her articles reveals that Alexandra David considered the relationships between men and women in purely physiological terms, discounting any spiritual or emotional conception of both marriage and motherhood.[196] The anthropologist on whom she relied for her understanding of the various forms of marriage found in the world is Charles Letourneau (1831-1902), one of the founders of the *Société d'anthropologie de Paris* who developed a materialistic, evolutionist and racist view of the human being, in the fashion of the time. The book she cites is Letourneau's *L'évolution du mariage et de la famille* (1888), in which the author explains that all human habits regarding love, marriage and family are only hypocritical inventions aimed at imposing domination by certain individuals (mostly men) over others (mostly women) and at hiding the crude fact that what really happens between men and women – who are nothing but tamed animals – is seasonal rut.

The crude nature of love and procreation is the reason why some intelligent women understand they have better things to do than conceive and educate children. Alexandra David considers that the rational feminist should have the choice not to reproduce. The women who wish to do something else, something more intellectual with their lives, should be able to renounce motherhood. The advice she gives her women readers is to retreat from the sexual realm altogether (to remain virgins) and to gain economic independence.[197] Those who were "forced" to have children or who realized later that they had no maternal inclinations should be able to give their offspring to the State, which would educate them honestly, even if it is with no warmth. Better the cold hands of the State than a miserable home with a negligent or violent mother.[198]

Alexandra David, who in her late-1900s writings exhibits clear socialist leanings, was one of the first feminists of her time to advocate for such a choice[199] in a society that had no contraception devices or birth control policies, nor any notion that women could choose not to be mothers. The other feminists of the time, who belonged to the previous generation, such as the author and freemason Maria Deraismes (1828-1894), the political activist Louise Michel (1830-1905), and the writer André Léo (1824-1900), mostly advocated for women's civil and political rights.

However, despite her disdain and apparent disgust for men, her own rational feminist strategy to get what her society would not give her (since she had no personal fortune, contrary to other feminists like Deraimes and Durand) was to marry one of her lovers, Philippe Néel, a wealthy client of the casino in Tunis where she sang, in 1904 – and leave him a few years later to start her famous journeys East, at his expense. Here we get a more precise understanding of what Louise David meant by rational. She meant rational egoist, in the idiom of her then-master, Max Stirner. This definition of the word is of paramount importance, as it is the first adjective which she uses to describe Buddhism – what she calls a "rational philosophy."

5

IN THE BUDDHA'S MOTHERLAND

You will never explain the religious traditions of the Greeks and the Latins, the things that are taught under the name of "mythology," if you do not look for their primitive forms where they are, that is to say in the Veda. It is also there that you will find the origin of the Northwestern peoples, of the Germans, the Celts, the Scandinavians… The great, the true story is the one that tells what is essential, what is fundamental in humanity: and that is above all the religious idea… The Veda is without a doubt one of the first sources of the religious idea, at least in the Aryan race from which we come… India may explain it, but on one condition: that we decide to ask India and understand the answers she left in her writings. Then, or so I hope, will the golden chain of human thought that runs from Aristotle and Plato to Voltaire and Descartes be reconnected for us to the Veda.

Émile-Louis Burnouf
***De la nécessité des Études Orientales*, 1861**

THE ORIENTALIST REPORTER

Louise David, who had also been known as Alexandra Myrial, Sasha, Mitra and Sunyananda, was now Alexandra David-Néel. With this new and stable identity, she became famous around the world as an intrepid explorer of Tibet and a prolific writer on Oriental topics. When she started her travels in 1911, however, her career was far from successful. In the early 1900s she had abandoned her singing career, a profession she found too precarious and too dependent on men's sexual appetites.[200]

She had wanted to start a new career as a novelist. Trying to get her two novels published, she had frequented some of the most fashionable literary circles, including the salon of the feminist writer Rachilde (Marguerite Eymery), the wife of the founder of the prestigious literary journal *Le Mercure de France*. This, too, had failed, and she became increasingly depressed. Her unpublished correspondence with her husband between 1904 and 1911 shows how industrious she was in Paris, trying to rework and sell her texts in slightly different form, meeting with publishers and as many useful contacts as possible, while trying to cope with chronic insomnia, headaches, digestive disorders, and gloom.[201] No treatment, no doctor, no water cure seemed to improve her condition, and her "neurasthenia" remained one of the main topics of discussion between her and her husband. She thought she needed a radical change, so when Philippe suggested she spend several months in India and the Far East at his expense she immediately agreed.[202]

For her, the trip was also an occasion to "renew her stock of knowledge" and write other, more original books and articles on Asian cultures, giving herself a second chance as a "woman of letters."[203] By 1911 she had published over 30 articles on Eastern religions and various political subjects, plus her anarchist manifesto and three books on Asian philosophers (Mozi, Yang Zhu, and the Buddha).[204] She was known in cultivated Parisian circles as a knowledgeable person on Asian cultures but was most probably considered an eccentric by French academic institutions. In any case, she was never able to launch a scientific career. Whether sincere or just trying to rationalize her rejection by academia, she claimed to have a completely original approach to Asian studies, an approach that professional scholars were unable to comprehend or accept.

In a letter to her husband written on board the *Mishima Maru*, which transported her to India, she says: "My stock of knowledge to spread is exhausted. I need to renew it, to stretch it, so that I can offer the public something other than repetitions and banalities. There is a very honourable place to take in French Orientalism [Asian studies], a more prestigious and more interesting place than that of our specialists, confined in their dry and dead erudition. I found that this place was for me. If my perseverance and hard work are sufficient, I need only take it. I saw – and I was not dreaming – a crowd coming to my conferences in Paris, the large audience that I gathered in Brussels, and, in S. Lévi's drawing room, men deserting the corner where one was expertly conversing to join and hear me talk about living Hindu philosophy, which is not preoccupied with the date and place of birth nor even the historical existence or non-existence of great thinkers, but considers ideas in themselves, from wherever they come, seeing them as manifestations of humanity's brain rather than the doctrines invented by X or Y, and relying on them, not to slavishly copy the forms that they have taken in the past, but to make them a fulcrum that allows our generation to go forward and further."[205]

In other words, true to herself and to Léon de Rosny's teachings, she was more interested in an ideological rather than a scientific approach to Asian doctrines. If she published articles in scholarly journals, it was primarily to earn a little money and establish her legitimacy as a writer and thinker. Her aim was not to know for the sake of knowing, but to absorb and present to readers any Oriental doctrine that could be of interest for social reformers and intellectuals. She was still influenced by her counter-cultural training in occultist-socialist societies. She wished to build a new temple, and Hindu, like Chinese, "philosophies" tended to serve as mere construction tools.

It is this ideological interest in Asian thought that had led her to write her book on Buddhism, published just before she departed for India, and a few years earlier her two books on the moral and political doctrines of Mozi (around 479-390 BC) and Yang Zhu (around 350 BC). These two ancient Chinese philosophers, whom she probably heard of at the Guimet Museum or in Parisian academic circles, appealed to her because they had developed views of humanity and society similar to hers.

Mozi was presented as a precursor of Socialism, a thinker and political activist from humble origins who challenged the hierarchical family-based model of society promoted by Confucius and proposed to reorganize the State based on more rational principles and on the notion of "universal love." Yang Zhu, on the other hand, was described in her article as "a Chinese Stirner," a strong proponent of individualism.[206]

Although different and in many ways in complete opposition, these two thinkers were incarnations of the two political traditions to which David-Néel had belonged in her twenties and early thirties. They also illustrate her understanding of "rationality." Indeed, both thinkers considered that the key to a harmonious individual and social life was not the pursuit of virtue (an idea taught by Confucius and European conservatives alike) but the legitimate satisfaction of each person's needs – a belief she had drawn from her readings of anarchist thinkers, in particular Max Stirner, and which she had expressed a few years earlier in *Pour la vie* (1900).

Mozi and Yang Zhu's thinking could demonstrate that the modern ideological systems called Socialism and Anarchism in the West were in fact ancient constructs. Appearing five centuries before our era in the great Chinese civilization, they were perhaps far superior to what most Europeans thought of them – and were very much needed. These two books, however, did not sell well, and she hoped to find more lucrative subjects for her next publications.

David-Néel was now willing to take advantage of her Eastern travels to find and collect new examples of exotic philosophical doctrines that could serve both her literary career and her reformist ambitions. She was especially interested in Vedanta, for several reasons: it was a Hindu philosophy that was both ancient and still alive, it was considered by many scholars to have a link with Buddhism (it was believed to have influenced Northern Buddhism, accounting for the presence of the supernatural in Mahayana traditions), and it was an area of study in which she could challenge French academia with contemporary ethnographic data.[207]

In fact, Vedanta was the Hindu philosophical tradition that appealed most to Westerners in the early 20th century, not only for its intrinsic qualities and the way it matched many intellectuals' expectations (it can account for religious diversity while offering the assurance that every human being could find the divine within in one lifetime through correct knowledge and the practice of yoga), but also because this tradition was being promoted on an international level by Hindu reformists such as Swami Vivekananda (1863-1902). A decade before, the latter had caused a sensation at the Chicago Parliament of World Religions (1893) with a speech on universality, harmony among religions, and tolerance – themes mostly inspired by his masonic and philosophical training with Westerners and, not surprisingly, appealing to his American audience.

The founder of the Ramakrishna Mission, which aimed at promoting Vedanta and celebrating the memory of his late master Ramakrishna (1836-1886), Vivekananda also contributed to the evolution of Hindu nationalism, together with other contemporary thinkers like Rabindranath Tagore, Sri Aurobindo and Gandhi. This political dimension of the Hindu revival greatly interested David-Néel, as her famous journalistic memoir about India testifies.[208]

It is probably through her Theosophical connections that David-Néel became aware of these Hindu reformists and decided to go to India and meet them. In a letter to her husband, she writes that she met Vivekananda in Paris in 1900 at a congress on the history of religions but did not quite like him.[209] The bad impression she got of him, however, did not damage her desire to write about the contemporary Hindu scene. More precisely, her plan was to write a book on Vedanta that would be both erudite and lively. She would study and translate texts from the Sanskrit with the help of teachers she would recruit through her Theosophical networks and interview leaders of the Hindu revival movement. She already had a title for the book, *Vedanta contemporain* (Contemporary Vedanta), and after a few months of exploration she decided to write a second book that she planned to title *L'Inde mystique* (Mystical India).[210]

The latter project took four decades and several additional journeys to complete, for she unexpectedly became caught up with her study of (and public association with) Tibetan Buddhism. The book on India was finally published in 1951 as *L'Inde. Hier, aujourd'hui, demain* (India: Yesterday, Today, Tomorrow), and was reedited in 1969 as *L'Inde où j'ai vécu* (India Where I Lived).[211]

The book on modern Vedanta was never completed. It was replaced by two French translations of Vedantic poems, also published much later: *Astavakra Gita: Discours sur le Vedanta Advaita* (Astavakra Gita: Discourse on Advaita Vedanta) in 1951, and *Avadhuta Gita de Dattatraya: Poème mystique Vedanta advaita* (Avadhuta Gita of Dattatraya: Advaita Vedanta Mystical Poem) in 1958.[212]

It seems she became more interested in depicting Hindu religious ideas and practices, which she termed "the mental life"[213] or "the psychical landscapes of India."[214] She quickly understood that the picturesque and, to a European eye, extravagant and often shocking Indian religious life offered far better writing material than the sophisticated philosophical theories professed by the Vedantists. Her new objective as an orientalist reporter thus became the creation of "a series of portraits showing the mental life rather than the material life of India."[215] The scholarly study and translation of Sanskrit texts became increasingly accessory, a work she felt compelled to do if she were to gain some scientific credibility.

The journalistic part of her new career might have been suggested by the contemporary birth of the modern, professional *grand reportage*, a literary genre that not only allowed for the bounteous description of exotic countries and peoples, but also highlighted the personality, style and courage of the author. These multifaceted aspects of the profession, combining far-away journeys, the opportunity to display a flamboyant personality, a taste for adventure, and an inclination toward literary rather than purely factual writing must have bolstered her sense of self-worth.

Being an orientalist reporter was not only about travelling, nor was it just about writing; it was about creating a whole new romantic character out of oneself. David-Néel had enjoyed being an actress and had created literary alter-egos in her novels, so she probably liked the prospect of playing another part and creating a new *mise-en-scène* for herself. The fact that she was not employed by any newspaper as their *grand reporter*, however, makes it difficult to call David-Néel, at this point in her life, a journalist in the strict sense of the word – though she did sell some of her manuscripts to several newspapers and journals. As an independent writer, she was about to create a unique type of *reportage*, which may be termed Theosophical reportage.

The Psychical Landscapes of India

David-Néel did not publish a travel diary so, with her books on India and Tibet rarely giving clear indication of places and dates, it is difficult to contextualize her Indian writings. She wrote about religious themes, did character portraits, told stories and anecdotes that seem truthful and grounded in personal experience, but she did not provide much historical data. Where and when did she meet that particular *guru*? Where and when did she attend that colourful ritual? What itinerary did she follow? How much time did she spend in that special place? What method did she use to meet her informants and become accepted by the diverse sects she describes?

It is often difficult to tell, and the general absence of such information distances her work from journalistic or ethnographic standards. Fortunately, we can get a clearer idea about her journeys in the letters she sent her husband, which were not only a way to keep in touch with him but were also consciously conceived as some kind of fieldwork notes to be safeguarded and used later.

David-Néel arrived in India via Ceylon. She spent three months there (9 August-16 November 1911), mainly staying in Colombo and Kandy. She frequented Theosophists and used their accommodations and personal networks to facilitate her stay and her studies. She notably visited her Theosophist friends at the Maha Bodhi Society, an organization founded in Colombo in 1891 by the Sri Lankan Buddhist leader Anagarika Dharmapala and the British journalist and poet Edwin Arnold to restore ancient Buddhist shrines in India. On 10 September she participated in an event organized by the Buddhist Theosophical Society to celebrate the opening of a girls' school. She also took Sanskrit lessons with Nyanatiloka, a German Buddhist convert who became a Bikkhu in Ceylon, and she visited important Buddhist places such as the Buddha's tooth relic temple in Kandy and the Bodhi Tree in Anuradhapura,[216] making this part of her trip her second pilgrimage.

She then spent four months in India (17 November 1911-27 March 1912), visiting Madurai, Rameswaran (an important pilgrimage destination), Trichinopoly (now Tiruchirappalli, famous for its Ganesh temple), Pondicherry, Madras (where she stayed at the Theosophical headquarters in Adyar, a place she describes as a very comfortable "lunatic asylum" and "a little Sodom led by the prophet Leadbeater"),[217] and Calcutta.

In Southern India, she was especially interested in Vaishnava and Shiva temples, which she managed to visit during religious ceremonies through her recent connections with a Brahman family. It was actually on a train in November 1911 that she made her first connection with a local Brahman, who enabled her to discover "mystical India" off the Theosophical beaten track. The event is famous and has been depicted in many biographies and movies as an illustration of David-Néel's capability to impress the natives with her spiritual knowledge.

The meeting happened by chance, "a fat Brahman" having entered her train compartment "very politely asked if he could travel with [her]."[218] She agreed and they soon engaged in conversation: "Soon after his arrival in my compartment, he started to talk about some banality that I cannot remember... oh yes! it was about the electric ventilator that had suddenly started to function by itself... And because I was coming from Rameswaran we talked about gods, and then about philosophy. With a Hindu, one always comes to this topic, and very quickly.

"At some point, because I was looking for a quote, I picked up the *Bhagavad Gita* from my bag, and immediately I conquered my travelling companion's esteem. I told him what the goal of my journey was, and he told me that if I wanted to spend the next day at his place in Madurai he would ask the professor who explains the Vedas in the temple to come over so I can speak to him. The proposal was too tempting for me to refuse."[219]

She then spent the next day in the house of the Brahman who, she discovered with some disappointment, happened to be "a kind of solicitor." However trivial his profession, it is through him that she could get access to some of the religious realms that were usually closed to Westerners. She describes her first discussion with the two men in the solicitor's personal shrine as a kind of mysterious initiation bestowed to her by virtue of her intellectual superiority: "Imagine a patio closed with four round columns, thinner at the base than at the top. A yellow curtain closes one side, and below this curtain one can see the feet of a couch, a piece of white cover, suspended clothes. It must be the master's bedroom. Before the curtain, a swing suspended by iron chains painted in black bears a cushion. Another side [of the patio] is shut by Turkey red screens, above which appear heads of people watching with curiosity. The third side forms a passage from the street to the house, and on the fourth we are seating around a table covered with a piece of raspberry-coloured cotton fabric and supporting a book-shaped box of betel. In this setting where hints of temple fragrances float – the same that are burnt on the family shrine – jasmine, incense, rancid oil and butter, we talk about those things that are inexpressible in our Western languages and which, fortunately, are familiar to me under their Sanskrit names.

"Once again, I asked the questions that agitated Yajnâvalka and Arthabaya in the distant ages and my Brahmans who, by the way, did not find more answers than those far away ancestors, were delighted by the sole sonority of syllables that their race repeat for generations and generations. Delighted to hear them manipulated, not without dexterity, by a Western woman. And so they forgot their usual reserve, repeating, in front of me, the sacred Mantrams, discussing their meaning and their virtue, unveiling the mysteries of chutram [sutra?], forbidden to all, except the Brahmans. I knew what this sanctuary was hiding, heart of the temple, surrounded by so many corridors, shrines, and gods; but very few non-initiates know this detail that must not be disclosed. The sanctuary of sanctuaries is divided into two parts by a wide curtain. By way of a worship, the Brahman lights a piece of camphor on a plate, he raises a corner of the curtain and the quick fire that projects its light behind the saint veil lights no statue, no object, for behind the curtain there is nothing... The room that the faithful call the gods' dwelling is an empty room. One must not know that; there is the secret, the initiation... It is terribly symbolic."[220]

She explains that the two Brahmans did not hesitate to communicate the secret to her, making her – or rather recognizing her as – an initiate because they knew she was a Buddhist and, they thought, "Buddhists understand those things the same way we do."[221] The description she gives of what could have been a simple – if important – discussion between an ethnographer and her informants reminds us of the Sanskrit lessons she took at the Theosophical Society back in Paris. It shows how much she was still influenced by occultism at that time. The initiation theme, with all its binary vocabulary (the profane/the initiates, the outside of the temple/the heart of the temple, to veil/to unveil, obscurity/light, the apparent/the profound meaning of Sanskrit syllables and of the temple disposition and contents) appears in her letters from the East for the first time here, and this remained a dominant filter through which she sees and writes about India and Tibet.

This ensured her success as a *de facto* Theosophist writer. Her Theosophism, however, was original since, despite her deep interest in initiation and psychic phenomena, she considered ultimate reality to be empty, godless and without meaning. As a consequence of her double training in esotericism and materialism, she developed a very original way of looking at Eastern religions, as the excerpt above suggests. "Mystical India" is a kind of gigantic and multifaceted theatrical play, told by many idiots, full of sound and fury and ultimately signifying nothing, except for a few intelligent people (the initiates), who know there is nothing to know.

The Theosophical Society played a big part in David-Néel's travels, providing her with the lenses through which to see the Hindus and, more practically, also offering a valuable network of people and a most convenient place to stay. David-Néel spent an entire month in the Society's headquarters in Adyar (Madras), where she not only had cheap, clean and spacious rooms, but where she also met people she had long wished to meet. Among them was Lakshmi Narasu, about whom she had written enthusiastically in her article and in her book about Buddhist Modernism. It seems that Narasu was somehow in close contact with the Theosophists in Madras, so they could easily meet as soon as she arrived in Madras. She writes her husband that she was glad to meet him but found his house disgusting ("At his house, it is the most complete barbarity. I took a meal there and I promised myself never to do it again. The servants really have grubby manners.") and regretted that his wife was so "native" ("She had her little girls' noses pierced to introduce jewels in, and the poor daddy, who teaches physics in high school and is very learned, is powerless, drowned, as he says, in his entourage.")[222] She wrote nothing further about him or their philosophical exchanges, so it seems she was a little disappointed in her modernist hero.

Another influential person she met through the Theosophical Society was John George Woodroffe (1865-1936). An English advocate of the Calcutta High Court, Woodroffe studied Sanskrit and became a Yoga practitioner and a famous esoteric writer under the name of Arthur Avalon. Woodroffe was an advocate of Hinduism and, according to David-Néel, actively participated in "ecstatic" Tantric rituals with his wife and local Hindus while he was in Calcutta. In the 1910s and 1920s, Woodroffe published several books explaining Yogic practices to Westerners. One of the most famous is *The Serpent Power* (1919) in which he describes how the "kundalini" energy works in "the subtle bodies," how the chakras are organized, what they symbolize and how they work, how one can activate the circulation of the kundalini through the body's "channels" and reach blissful illumination.

His work could be described as overtly esoteric: "Arthur Avalon" (a symbolic name inspired by the Grail legend) was published by occultist publishers, his books written in a technical language characteristic of Theosophists and other occultists. Drawing both from his Theosophist background and from genuine Hindu texts and traditions, Woodroffe wished to make sense of Yogic and Shaktic practices in rational terms, so that they could appear as something more valuable than the spectacular, overemotional and inherently absurd behaviors they were to most of his compatriots. He showed that they were a perfectly coherent and meaningful set of techniques, based on a profound philosophy and on an empiric conception of the human body. His work had a great influence on Indology and on popular culture alike but remained too imbued with Western esotericism to be taken seriously by academia.

Woodroffe, in any case, provided David-Néel with easy access to certain confidential rituals, which she describes in *L'inde où j'ai vécu*. She does not mention his name in her book, but there is a clear reference to Woodrooffe in her chapter on Shaktism: "If I dared tackle a delicate subject, I would reveal that I knew of a European, a scholar who belonged to his country's high society, who was a shakta. What was he looking for with the Goddess [Shakti]? He confessed to me that he saw in the shakta ritual a sort of magic and that he thought he could get material profit out of it. He used to participate in mystical *tchakras* [sic], of irreproachable purity.

As for his wife, with whom he was very much in love, he regarded her as the Goddess, and before their intimate *maithuna* [ritual sexual relation], he adored her as one adores the image of Shakti in the temples, swaying flowers and ritual lamps with multiple little flames before her, as well as burning incense while chanting Sanskrit hymns."[223] Mrs. Woodroffe also proved to play an important part in David-Néel's travels: she introduced her to certain circles of English expatriate high society – these circles, boring though they were, proved to be very useful when David-Néel needed travel authorizations or political protection.

David-Néel could also count on her French occultist connections to meet important players in the Hindu revival. It was through her friend Mirra Alfassa, then Madame Richard, that she met Aurobindo Ghose. Mira Alfassa (1878-1973), who remained a friend of David-Néel's throughout her life, was a French painter of Levantine Jewish descent who, in her twenties, met with a mysterious Polish Jewish occultist known as Max Théon, and through him became interested in Kabbalah, channelling, occultism and Oriental philosophies. She gave up painting and decided to dedicate her life to the elucidation of psychic phenomena and the pursuit of Truth. First married to symbolist artist Henri Morisset, a disciple of Gustave Moreau, Mirra Alfassa separated from her husband, who did not approve of her new esoteric activities. She remarried Paul Richard, a diplomat and philosopher, whom she met in Orientalist Parisian circles. Together they started a philosophical quest that led them to meet Aurobindo in 1914 in Pondicherry, where Paul Richard, as a diplomat, had business to conduct.

Aurobindo was staying in the town, then French territory, to escape the British who tried to arrest him again for illegal political activity and murder. Aurobindo, who had been educated in England from a very early age, reconciled with his parents' culture, came back to India, became a radical political activist and was involved in terrorism. After spending some time in jail, where he later wrote that Vivekananda appeared to him, Aurobindo managed to reach Pondicherry, where he spent the rest of his life in secluded safety.

There, he developed his philosophy, which he called Integral Yoga or Integral Vedanta. Those teachings were based on the Darwinian theory of evolution, to which he added a spiritual dimension: man had not only evolved from monkey to his modern state, but he was also growing spiritually and would one day reach another level, giving birth to "a new, superior race." This belief, typical of 19th-century European occultist and socialist utopias, took on a Hindu coloration in his synthesis.[224]

He quickly started to attract disciples, called himself Sri Aurobindo – "Shri" being an honorific title – and in 1926 founded the Sri Aurobindo Ashram. Mirra Richard met Aurobindo in his little house in Pondicherry with her husband in 1914. Both immediately fell under his spell, especially Mrs. Richard, who recognized the Hindu man she had seen in a dream and bowed before a few years earlier. His energy, his aura, was irresistible. She nonetheless left Pondicherry to follow her husband to his next post in Japan. She remained there six years but was unhappy and returned to Pondicherry, where she spent the rest of her extraordinary life.

Mirra Alfassa became Aurobindo's spiritual consort, was elevated to the status of a living goddess, had thousands of disciples, lived in exquisite luxury, and was known as The Mother. Aurobindo and she made "a divine couple." He wrote his deep philosophy, while she put it into practice in the ashram, which she managed with authority and efficiency. The ashram became a little industry, selling a range of products that included handmade clothes and perfume. Mirra Alfassa also received important donations and was able to buy more than half of the colonial neighbourhood of Pondicherry, which became a gigantic ashram. The latter was conceived as a laboratory to experiment on "the new species" under a strict social and quasi-military regimen built around the personality cult of The Mother.

In the revolutionary year of 1968, the ninety-year-old French goddess expanded her Hindu kibbutz into an entire experimental town called Auroville (Dawn City), near Pondicherry. Attracting many young people from Europe and the United States, it was (and still is) dedicated to the establishment of human unity and to bringing about a new human race. The project received support from the Indian State and from UNESCO.[225]

David-Néel met Aurobindo three years before the Richards did, in November 1911. She had met the Richards in Paris a few years before she left for India and, she says, they recommended she meet him.[226] When she arrived in India, Aurobindo was already staying in Pondicherry. She says that when she arrived at his place, she was met by the chief of the English police, who came in person to meet her and already knew where she was staying, what she had done, and whom she had seen. The policeman told her that Aurobindo was a dangerous activist, involved in the murder of a British official. She replied that she had heard he was a great philosopher and that was why she was visiting him. She also showed him the letters of recommendation she got from the London Indian Office, which seemed to reassure the Englishman.[227]

She wrote her husband: "I had a meeting with a Hindu… I spent two hours to stir the ancient philosophical ideas of India with an interlocutor of such rare intelligence, who belonged to this uncommon race that has all my sympathy: the reasonable mystics. I am so grateful to those friends who advised me to go and meet this man. He thinks with such neatness, there is so much lucidity in his reasoning, such radiance in his gaze that he gives you the impression to have contemplated India's genius in the highest pages of Hindu philosophy."[228]

Three months later, in February 1912 after staying several weeks in Calcutta, she returned to Pondicherry to get new letters of recommendation. She thought she could take the opportunity to visit Aurobindo again but for some reason was not able to do so. She writes: "I did not suspect this man was so important. If I had known, I would have tried to make him talk about politics, to know what kind of ideas can spring in the brain of a Vedantic mystic. But, although I knew he had had a political trial, I did not exactly know the reason for it. This morning I saw the king's private secretary, who told me: 'I think he finds our civilization, our education, and all our progress too *godless* [original in English], which means 'without God' and for this reason reproves them.' This could be true. The Hindus see things and the world from a very different angle. I could, maybe, if our meeting had not been confined to the twilight hours, in his monastic house of Pondicherry, have found out what, in this brain, was the crack in our Western, materialistic world... and I could have done an interesting study of a foreign mentality... Yes, this could have been very interesting... The dissection room with its debris of human organism is very interesting too... But, alas..."[229]

The rest of the letter is unclear but refers to her recollection of the evening she met Aurobindo, of the way they "talked about the Supreme Brahman, of eternal existence" and "dreamt the Uppanishads' dreams." In *L'Inde où j'ai vécu*, written several years later when she was aware of Aurobindo's importance, she devotes several pages to him, remembering their conversation, presenting his philosophy, and describing the ashram's functioning, based on the report of a friend who spent some time there.[230]

From the beginning of January to the end of March 1912, David-Néel mostly remained in Calcutta. She stayed in a boarding house run by a certain Mrs. Walters. "All this is very English," she writes her husband, "the exotic has gone."[231] She describes herself as "fallen back into civilization" with all the social duties that go with it. She was asked to lunches, teas and dinners by British people who were either distant relations, total strangers or freemason brothers. She was struck to see how similar to London Calcutta had become, "except for the crowd in colourful rags." She visited the Kalighat Kali Temple with "a French friend" she does not name, and in her letters describes how disgusted she was by the sacrifices practiced there: "We rolled our skirts up to our calves, literally wading in ponds of blood. What an ugly channel!"[232]

She also visited the Sanskrit College, an academic institution founded in 1824 on the advice of two English scholars, James Prinsep, an orientalist and antiquary who also founded the *Journal of the Asiatic Society of Bengal*, and Thomas Babington Macaulay, a British historian and Whig politician. She describes the college as "an archaic dream" with "vast and high rooms paved with marble. Carpets are laid here and there, most of them blue and white with stripes like Arabic blankets. In the middle of the carpet is a little flat mattress, a huge cylindrical cushion, and the whole thing is covered with white slipcovers… This is the chair on which the master sits, in the posture of my living room Buddha. Around the mattress, the students are gathered in circles, in the same pose. Among those scholars, some have very ordinary looks, and one would rather like to see them seated on chairs, but some are typical.

"The professor who teaches Vedanta is especially remarkable. He is a very tall man, slim without being skinny, with a very white face (a real Aryan Brahman from the North) and a high forehead on which the sectarian mark of the Vaishnava, a sort of V, is painted. I would very much like to photograph him with his students, squatting on his mattress. But making photographs in a room, lighted though it is, does not give much result."[233]

She is proud to announce to her husband that she was personally invited by the head of the school, who addressed her "with honours" and "sent a note to the newspapers to recount [her] visit and mention that [she] had had conversations of the highest interest with the professors." She was indeed "treated as a little highness" and "a very famous poet improvised Sanskrit verses to honor [her]." She was "compared to Saraswati, the goddess of Knowledge," but she notes that on the other hand the professors of Sanskrit, "the equivalent of our Collège de France or Sorbonne's professors," are treated by their principal as she "treats [her] boys."[234]

At the Sanskrit College she was able make the acquaintance of professors, some of whom agreed to come to her lodgings and "discuss Shankarâcharya's theories with [her]." She was disappointed by what she heard, however: "It is strange to see how personal thinking is unknown in India. When one listens to different people talking about these things, one has the impression of hearing a phonograph repeating the very same words. It is a hopeless monotony."[235] She nonetheless valued the help of the "pandits" to translate Sanskrit texts, probably the two Vedanta poems she later published.[236]

David-Néel also visited the local offices of the Brahmo Samaj, a syncretic movement founded in 1828 to reform Hinduism, which she compares to a Protestant church: "There, it smells like Protestantism, it is like being among the Unitarians… in a different setting of course. Nothing of the clear and neat room that was the church of my youth: the Hindu dirt is everywhere, as attenuated as possible, but present enough to surprise the Westerners, for the Brahmos recruit only among the highest classes of society. There are no popular elements among them, which is also the case among scholars. One sits on benches on the patio's balconies and one discusses. Before me sit half a dozen old men, the Church's missionaries. We are far from the transcendent intellectuality of the Vedanta, far from the Samâdhi that raises Chidambaram's veil, far from the smile of those who went beyond the theories, morals, religions, and gods… We are among the believers according to the old formula, similar to that of our Christians, although with more eclecticism and a sovereign tolerance which, without their noticing, still conveys some scepticism. Yes, we are far from the clear, slightly fearful, rather bitter thought of philosophical India, but there is, on the other hand, a spirit of practical sanctity, of charity, of real social progress that fail the Vedantists, isolated in their ivory tower. The Brahmos are the pioneers of all the generous reforms of India."[237]

A few days later she attended a service by one of the Brahmo Samaj branches. She logged her impressions in a detailed report: "It is quite a temple, and when I entered I had an impression of satisfaction and comfort that gives a familiar ground. The minister, too, smells terribly of the clergyman – too much, in this country of exuberant gods. He is not an orator, and he lingers on prayers that tire the assistants' attention. I look at the faces, in the audience. Some look very intelligent. Those who are here belong to the liberal elite of the nation, but this does not prevent most of them from being dressed in the most neglected way. A Westerner, uninformed, would readily think he is among the poor. Before me, a man draped in orange wool, is absorbed in his devotions. His face is very white, his hair and beard very dark, with eyelashes falling down his cheeks. He is very handsome, very artistic, and very impressive in his mystical rapture… I look at him with pleasure, as an artistic delight… but then my beautiful statue comes out of his dreams and blows his nose in his sumptuous orange draperies."[238]

On January 12, 1912 she spent the day at the Belur Math, the monastery and headquarters of the Ramakrishna Mission, founded by Vivekananda in 1897. It is in the letter she writes afterwards that she expresses her dislike of Vivekananda and also gives a colourful description of the activities that took place on the latter's birthday: "Yesterday, I spent my day at the Belur Math, among the disciples of the late Vivekananda, whose birthday they celebrated. I am always very cordially welcome at the Math, and this time what I saw was very curious. Hundreds of people arrived and filled the gardens where meals were offered to the poor, coming from all sides. A kitchen has been installed under a makeshift shelter, bags of rice are poured on mats, twenty gigantic cauldrons are full of various curries and cook on piles of wood. This is for the material part. As for the spiritual, there is a kind of flowerbed, under a thatched mushroom like those we put in our parks. In the middle of the flowerbed, garlanded with yellow chrysanthemums, is a great portrait of the late master in sannyâsin costume; orange drapery, the danda or pilgrim stick in hand, the haughty, vain, almost arrogant look he had during his lifetime and that he carried with him in Europe and America.

"He was a great orator, an impulsive, a mentally disordered person, jumping from one thought to another. He had a few impulses towards generosity and light, but they were only brief sparks, quickly extinguished… All his life he remained a reactionary, the man with the dry heart he was during his famous speech to Madras' gentlemen on his return from America. I did not like him in his lifetime and to find him here in an apotheosis does not incline me to much more sympathy.

"Nevertheless, in front of the image, squatting in semicircles, a chorus of young men are chanting, marking the rhythm with a small bell with a silvery tinkle. They are singing, in Sanskrit, very old and famous hymns by Sankarâcharya. I watched them from a balcony above. Shreds of sentences came to me and one of the swamis, who caught them too, translated to me what I did not understand: 'How can you believe that your Self is your body… How can you believe that your Self is your senses… Impermanent they are… Here is your passed youth, old age comes, and death will blow on your body and disperse your senses… Elsewhere is your eternal Self… Look for Brahman… Look for Brahman!'

"I asked to go up to the oratory, which is a little outside the rules, because strictly speaking only Hindus can penetrate this place. But one of the swamis said: 'Why would you not enter?' I removed my shoes and entered the little sanctuary. People are prostrating before a kind of throne where the picture of Sri Ramakrishna Paramahamsa rests. Before the throne are objects that belonged to him, and his ashes are on the throne itself. This is, in fact, a funerary chapel, clear and clean. In the forecourt, several religious pictures decorated the walls and I stayed in front of a Kali dancing on Shiva, very impressive, very telling, as was also the white Shiva lying under the fury's feet and looking at me behind his closed eyelids."[239]

She also visited the room where Ramakrishna lived, and three days later met with his widow, Saradadevi: "I went to see the widow of the deified man, Sri Ramakrishna Paramahamsa, whose room I had visited at the Dakshineshwar Temple and the Belur Chapel. To be in front of a god's wife! ... Those things happen only in India and are considered perfectly natural. It is in a distant, difficult-to-find neighbourhood in a white house whose cleanliness is in sharp contrast to what one usually finds here. The ground floor is occupied by the Ramakrishna Mission's offices. The swami publisher lives there. He is a fat, genial, very simple man..." She explained that the swami offered to remove her shoes and that this behaviour had shocked his entourage.

She then went upstairs: "It is a chapel with a little throne, a canopy, and Sri Ramakrishna's picture like in Belur, but smaller. On the edge of a large plank bed, without mattress, the widow is sitting, all in white. According to Bengali custom, like that of the Muslims, she is hiding her face because the swami is not a parent of hers. When he left, and I was alone with her and my interpreter, who is from her family, the old lady shows me her face. It is a very pretty face, very young, extraordinarily young for a sixty-year-old Oriental woman. She has no wrinkles, and her eyes are the most beautiful in the world, full of intelligence and of life. I have rarely seen such an intelligent face among Hindu women. The conversation was naturally short, as is always the case with an interpreter, and then the good woman became terribly shy. I caught a few sentences of what the interpreter said, thanks to the consonance of Sanskrit words interposed in the Bengali discourse."[240]

Later, Saradadevi sent David-Néel a picture of herself, which she placed on her desk next to her husband's picture.[241] She had wanted to meet Margaret Noble, the Irish woman who had become a disciple of Vivekananda under the name of Sister Nivedita, but the latter had died a few months before in Darjeeling. David-Néel nonetheless visited the girls' school Margaret Noble had founded, now being run by an American woman.

David-Néel wrote her husband explaining how horrified she was by the Hindu custom of marrying off very young girls, which turned some of them into widows at age five, who were then unable remarry and often fell into prostitution or misery. She also mentioned that when espousing the Hindu faith, "Miss Noble" had also become so "blinded" as to "justify the worst social and religious horrors."[242] It seems that David-Néel was shocked by the treatment reserved for Hindu women, to the detriment of her original vision of "high Hindu philosophy."

In Calcutta, as elsewhere in India, she was also perplexed by the way Hindus treated the dead. She recounts how she saw a cadaver on the street, "turned pink like certain dolls made with skin, the head unrecognizable, the lips gnawed leaving the teeth bare,"[243] and how the Hindus did not care about it. She devotes many pages to the subject of funerary rites, either in her correspondence or in *L'Inde où j'ai vécu*. While trying to appear cool-headed and tolerant, she seems to have been shocked by what she witnessed (dead people on the street, bodies cut and burnt in charnel-houses, etc.). The caste system is also a topic she frequently addresses critically in *L'Inde où j'ai vécu*. To avoid trouble and be able to join various Hindu groups, she usually introduced herself as a Buddhist, a position that gave her considerable prestige and freedom. It also allowed her to reconcile, at least temporarily, people of different castes who wanted to spend time with her without sharing one another's meals. Indeed, when Brahmins did not want to mix with lower-caste people while meeting with her, she lectured them on the Buddha's rejection of the caste system, on selflessness and the inherently empty nature of things – and the Brahmins stopped asking for preferential treatment.[244]

She had come to India to assess the contemporary practice of Vedanta and was curious to see how so-called great Hindu philosophers were reforming the country's culture. After a few months there, her disillusion was obvious. She made it clear to her husband that she did not believe the Hindu reformists would establish a new, egalitarian, modern society in India. The Hindu reformists and political activists, she wrote in February 1912, "talk more than they act, and it is better that way, for most of those nationalists are just nasty reactionaries, not at all generous, progress-loving patriots, as is often believed. There must be some in that heap, that is for sure, but they are not the majority. If the English were expelled from India, it would be a terrible carnage and a return to barbarity."[245]

It is not what another famous French writer would say about India and its masters in the next decades. Romain Rolland (1866-1944), awarded the 1915 Nobel Prize of Literature, published several laudatory books on Gandhi, Ramakrishna and Vivekananda, which introduced these Hindu reformers to the French public in the most positive light. Because of Rolland's literary prestige and although he never set foot in India, his books tended to render David-Néel's criticism irrelevant.[246]

David-Néel's personality as a European intellectual and as a Brahman's friend, able to read Sanskrit and interested in ritual practices, attracted the attention of many ascetics and scholars from different sects who invited her to join their community or to adopt their lifestyle. In December 1911, for instance, while she was still in Madras, she was visited by three Vaishnava ascetics who invited her to train with them until she became sufficiently enlightened to go back to Europe and teach Westerners the Truth: "The scene happens in the great livingroom of the villa where I live in Adyar. They are three, in front of me, with their long caftans, their head turbaned with white chiffon embroidered with silver. On the dark skin of their forehead are painted the sectarian marks of the Vaishnavas. One of them has visibly borrowed the very sacred substance the cows naturally produce, without being aware, innocent as they are of the religious value of their digestion's residues. Their faces are hard, resolved as if they were going into battle, and it is indeed for a fight that they came…

"They want to offer me this thing perhaps never offered before to someone of my race and especially of my sex: the abandonment of everything, the sannyasin [ascetic's] life, among them until the day comes when, having realised the great realisation, Brahman, the unique, I will be able to teach the West what no scholar has ever managed to show: their saints and their philosophers' Great Vedanta. Yes, it was about throwing away my clothes, about living naked, or almost, under a shelter of some kind, without furniture or servants. It was about becoming a yogi according to the ancient formula, looking, not in books, but by oral initiations given by gurus, for the liberating moksha. Gently, I insinuated that somewhere, on another continent, lived a gentleman who was my husband and that, maybe, he would show very little enthusiasm for such an avatar of his wife."[247]

Several weeks later, while in Calcutta, she received an offer to live in a professor's quiet home free of charge for six months to learn Sanskrit and Hindu philosophy. The swamis she met at Belur, she said, made similar offers, as well as members of the Arya Samaj (the Noble Society), a Hindu reform movement that promoted a strict return to the Vedic scriptures.[248] She does not say why, but such a prospect was out of the question. Her continuous refusals confirm that she was not personally interested in such a spiritual quest. It was intellectual curiosity and the wish to write original books that motivated her.

In February 1912 she wrote her husband: "To go back to the topic of this journey, I would like your advice. What should I do? You realize, by the number of critical articles that my last book [*Le bouddhisme du Bouddha*] aroused and by the asperity of the fight the clerical clan started against me, that it is among the books that people attach importance to. My *Vedanta* might be even more 'sensational,' and the discussions I lead will put me very much in view. These situations require the support of appropriate erudition... My situation is difficult among the orientalists. They consider me a negligible quantity and will discuss my work. But I do not want to live in their shadow. I want to show what I saw, what I know by experience about Asian doctrines."[249]

What she saw and understood by experience while in India was published much later than it should have been.[250] The book is not a memoir about her own spiritual experience with Vedanta teachers, as one might have expected. It is very different from the letters she wrote her husband, which were both factual and personal. *L'Inde où j'ai vécu* is composed of "a series of pictures showing the mental life, rather than the material life, of India."[251] It is neither a chronological nor an ethnographical record of her Indian journeys but is more of a literary fresco based on her memories, with many vivid scenes and picturesque characters, most of the time undated and unnamed. The result is enjoyable and entertaining, often thoughtful and documented, but the rituals, scenes and religious authorities she describes are generally too disconnected from their historical background to be used as scientific data. The reader is left with the impression of being immersed in a timeless fictional, rather than realistic, document. Moreover, the lens through which she views "the Indian religious landscape" remains tinted with Theosophical concerns.

Her concerns include how the Hindus "animate" a statue (according to her by "transfusion of energy," the power of thought, which has imperceptible but effective material qualities).[252] How can one create "esoteric doubles," a phenomenon she says she later witnessed in Tibet (she even says she created *tulpa*, not a difficult thing to do)?[253] How can the practices of shaktic devotion and other magic-yogic practices help develop latent faculties and lead to the acquisition of "supernormal cerebral activity?"[254] How can one explain Aurobindo's "magnetism"[255] and the "super-mental light" he manifested at his death?[256] What is the "hypnotic" nature of the guru-student relationship?[257] And so on.

Another important theme she develops in this book has to do with initiations given in dark temples and leading to the discovery of nihilism, described in theatrical terms. She is also greatly interested in "lubricious" rituals (also called "rut Samadhi") which she depicts with polite coarseness, disgust and irony.[258] She also addresses theological questions such as: "How do Hindus conceive of their gods and see them?"[259] She gives a universal, materialistic explanation of the myriad gods that appear in real, material form to certain people, thus leading other people to believe literally in their existence – she notably cites the case of Ramakrishna and his little statue of Râmbâla, which according to some witnesses became a real living boy.[260]

She explains that the concentrated thought of many people on one object (in India, Durga or Krishna, in Europe, the Virgin Mary) produces an energy that is "absolutely not immaterial," and this energy produces a "hallucination." The latter is not an image that remains in each person's mind, but one that is projected on to reality just as a movie is projected on a screen. The transmitters of the image are hallucinating, i.e., they think of someone that does not exist (the deity), but the image they produce is itself real, materially imprinted on reality. Beliefs in gods, deities, saints, or other supernatural beings are therefore based as much on something real (the visible image) as on something immaterial (the image that one sees is ultimately the mere production of several minds playing together).[261] The scientific explanations she gives of the Hindus' religious beliefs and practices make this book a Theosophical one. Indeed, like other Theosophists (and many psychoanalysts), David-Néel believed that the human mind had faculties or powers that were not extraordinary or supernatural but simply unknown or unexplained. Her originality as a Theosophist, however, was to believe these unusual functions were purely physiological: the mind, for her, was simply the brain, a complex composition of cells, not a spiritual entity.

As a Theosophist writer, she was also unique in not adopting the stereotypically technical and dense prose other Theosophists used. Her style is very personal. She does not describe esoteric laws or the organisation of the human body in relation to the universe, as most occultists did. Instead, she describes people, scenes, situations that seemed curious or paranormal at first sight and then explains them with Voltairian irony: "strange facts and bizarre people" are often reduced to gross theatrical tricks designed by "fake teachers" or "professional gurus" to lure stupid people.

In any case, the book she dedicated to her Indian journeys only accidentally deals with Vedanta, her initial research topic. Instead, it is mainly concerned with the spiritually exotic – the beliefs and ritual practices that seemed strange to Europeans of the era, whether they considered them repulsive, comical or reprehensible. The book seems to illustrate the way she came to conceive of the world, probably after her training with Tibetan lamas who taught her the Yogacara doctrine. "Mystical India," like any other cultural reality, is the dancing "maya," the ever-changing, polymorphous illusion that only the fool dare to call "reality" and which is only a product of the (material) mind.

To access this theatrical world, and especially backstage, with all its tricks and strings, she employed special strategies: the extensive use of disguise (the orange robes of the sannyasin, the convenient saris and veils of the Brahman woman), role-playing (the Sanskrit scholar, the apprentice ascetic, the Buddhist teacher – probably the sincerest), and spying from behind a curtain (especially when sexual rituals are involved). Another theatrical technique she used was to provoke "fake gurus," often ridiculing them with a direct question or an impertinent challenge to bring down her interlocutor's mask and reveal his real personality. In addition to her materialism, her conception of the world as a theatre was another original twist she gave to her Theosophical writings. She used the same kind of approach in many of her books on Tibet and its religions.

6

Entering History through the Gates of Lhasa

> *What, then, is the dreadful charm of this strange country, where those who once glimpsed it have always returned? To meet again its mountains and its men, one crosses the sea, one crosses entire kingdoms, all China, at the slow pace of camels and mules. We arrive in the frozen deserts, so high that they no longer seem to belong to the earth.*
>
> **Jacques Bacot, *Le Tibet révolté*, 1912**

Louise David never intended to go to Tibet. In truth, she did not have a very high opinion of what at the time was called Lamaism, which was considered to be a degenerate and syncretic form of Indian Buddhism.[262] In 1904, at a time when she had never even set foot in Tibet nor met a single Tibetan, she had already published an article entitled *Le pouvoir religieux au Thibet*.[263] In it she summarizes the legends relating to the arrival of Buddhism in Tibet along with the calendrical and religious organization of Tibetan society, in all probability drawing on information picked up from lectures given by Philippe-Edouard Foucaux, whose courses she attended irregularly circa 1893.[264]

She explains that in her view the Tibetan people's apparent addiction to "magic" was due to their natural environment, principally stemming from the fact that they live literally with their heads in the clouds: "It would be difficult to find in another nation the traits which characterize the Tibetan mentality. Fanaticism, devoutness, religiosity are inadequate and misleading terms when used to characterize the true feelings and emotions conjured up by the literature and mores of the 'Land of Snows.' Rather, it would seem that by living so close to the heavens the inhabitants of this place have become accustomed to being in constant contact with the superhuman hosts that according to Fable reside there, and by a perpetually recurring miracle they endlessly relive that mythical time when the immortals descended from Mount Olympus to mix with mankind."[265]

Apparently, this belief in magic was already prevalent among the lower classes of society in Tibet before the introduction of Buddhism by an elite (Buddhist patriarchs) coming from India in the 7th century. "Magicians, necromancers of every possible kind who abounded in Tibet [at that time] must have been acutely displeased by the intrusion of a foreign doctrine which threatened the very source of their power and wealth. However, they could rest assured: the people of the 'Land of Snows' were far too attached to the primitive magic that underpinned their rituals to do without it.

"Time and time again, monarchs and religious reformers tried to root out the ancient superstitions. Their efforts were in vain, and Buddhism only managed to prevail in Tibet via its assimilation of the major part of indigenous beliefs and practices, even reinforcing them at a later stage by numerous elements borrowed from the Shaivist-yogic sects. In short, little more than the name Buddhism was conserved."[266]

She goes on to speak of "the lamaist church" and theocracy, she considers that Padmasambhava, the founder of Tibetan Buddhism, was venerated more "for being an eminent magician than an apostle of Buddhism," and that the Dalai Lama was an autocrat, "the living idol of Lhasa," a simple "instrument (puppet) in the hands of his entourage." In short, the Tibetans were seen to be no different from other Asiatic peoples observed during their mantras: primitive pseudo-Buddhists flaunting that other unfortunate trait – the Tibetan cult was organized along similar lines to the Catholic Church. In letters to her husband around the time she entered "Mongolian Asia, Yellow Asia" and had her meeting with the thirteenth Dalai Lama in April 1912, she uses such expressions as "a farce," "the yellow Pope" and "the Great Manitou."[267]

It was by pure chance that Louise David's travels led her to Tibet. As she explains in the account of her journey to Lhasa: "The following year [1911], finding myself near Madras, I learned that the ruler of Tibet, the Dalai Lama, had fled his country – at that time in revolt against China – and was living in the Himalayas. Tibet was not completely unknown to me. I had studied under Professor Ed. Foucaux, a Tibetologist (Tibetan specialist/scholar) at the Collège de France, and I had a passing knowledge of Tibetan literature. The reader will understand – I did not want to miss this unique opportunity to see for myself the king of the lamas and his court."[268] Furthermore, the Dalai Lama's unexpected stay at the gateway to Sikkam coincided with the preferred summer destination of many British colonials seeking a cooler, healthier climate in the mountains. Therefore, in March 1912 she set out from Calcutta for Darjeeling with a group of British settlers and then went on to Kalimpong, where the Dalai Lama was in residence.

She was more explicit about her motives and objectives when writing to her husband: "To return with a study of Lamaism conducted right under the Dalai Lama's nose would be a really fantastic achievement for an orientalist."[269] The following day, she wrote excitedly in the heat of the moment: "The deed is done, my dearest. I met the yellow Pope this morning – a cordial reception, insofar as cordiality is able to exist between people of such differing cultures and mentality."

She goes on to fill in the details by describing her arrival at a palace that looked more like a "country chalet." "I was received with a great deal of curiosity with numerous pairs of slanted eyes staring at me. At the entrance, a Chamberlain greeted me. He was a little grubby but among the acolytes and servants that rushed to his side there were some whose clothing was so thickly coated in a layer of shiny grime that they looked as though they were dressed in bronze... Two Japanese dignitaries (visitors) had been granted an audience, and since it was understood that they would not stay long they were received before me and, sure enough, were swiftly despatched. We went upstairs. Laden La [Sonam Wangfel Laden, a Tibetan working for the Indian police who was in charge of helping with the 13th Dalai Lama's diplomatic agenda, opened the door and all of a sudden there I was in front of the Great Manitou himself. It all happened so quickly – I had expected there to be an antechamber – that I hesitated before bowing to the person seated on a simple chair by the window. But, as I had seen his portrait, I recognized him and greeted him."

She then relates the misunderstanding that prevailed among the attendees at the meeting. The Dalai Lama and his court thought that their visitor had come as a Buddhist – albeit a rather original one – since she had been introduced as such. As a Buddhist, it seemed obvious to them that she would recognize in the person of the Dalai Lama not only an earthly ruler but also a spiritual authority and the incarnation of a divine being.

Consequently, she was expected to seek the divinity's blessing. But Louise David, a materialist with quite a different conception of Buddhism, was not inclined to show the slightest sign of devotion towards the "Pontiff." She simply wanted to follow custom and usage to attain her objectives without shocking anyone, and in her view that consisted of curtsying and giving the Dalai Lama a traditional white silk scarf. These two acts she carried out and believed that she had acquitted herself by correctly observing the required etiquette, when her interpreter, quite amazed that she had simply given the scarf without expecting to receive the Dalai Lama's blessing in return, manifested his astonishment and immediately forced her to bow her head.

In this way she received the Dalai Lama's benediction simply by observing protocol so as to avoid an incident, while being careful to stress to her husband that it was only "play-acting." One should not therefore jump to the conclusion that this incident – the subject of numerous commentaries – meant that Louise David had taken (spiritual) refuge with the Dalai Lama in the Buddhist sense.[270]

After the Dalai Lama gave his blessing, they talked together. Their conversation is yet another illustration of the prevailing state of mutual astonishment and misunderstanding that characterized their encounter – as much concerning the true meaning of Buddhism as the implications of their meeting: "He naturally asked me the inevitable question – how long had I been a Buddhist and what had led me to Buddhism. But his Tibetan mind had the greatest difficulty in conceiving that one could become a Buddhist in a European university by virtue of (simply) studying Oriental philosophy. He could not comprehend the fact that I had neither a guru nor a teacher… and I left him feeling even more perplexed when I told him that, at the time of my conversion to Buddhism, I did not actually know a single Buddhist and that I was perhaps the only Buddhist in Paris. On hearing that, he laughed and told me that there indeed was an excellent reason for having gone without a teacher.

"We went on to talk about various matters. He seems to be naturally joyful and is certainly not an idiot, but no intellectual either in our sense of the word. His chamberlain or minister, a beanpole of a man, who did not stop babbling, looked to be far more on the ball. My host was quite obviously infatuated with his own importance, all the more so since the Chinese had done much to diminish the prestige that the Dalai Lama had previously enjoyed… The pontifical acolytes looked at me with both respect and amazement at having chatted for such a long time with the incarnation of Chenrési. I think all of this will make a nice little piece for the *Mercure*."[271]

Altogether the audience lasted for three quarters of an hour and among the attendees was the Buddhist monk Ekai Kawaguchi, famous for having entered Lhasa incognito. Louise David would meet him again sometime later in Japan, and it was almost certainly his idea that she should disguise herself as a beggar in order to gain access to the forbidden city. A second audience was agreed upon, during which Louise David would question the Dalai Lama on matters relating to Tibetan Buddhism.

Beforehand, she was to formulate her questions in writing, have them translated into Tibetan and then communicate them in advance. This second audition took place two months later, on June 25, 1912.[272] The two auditions were subsequently recounted in the form of a report that appeared in an issue of the *Mercure de France* published in October of the same year under the heading *Auprès du Dalaï Lama*.[273]

Although she passed herself off to her readers as being on close terms with the Dalai Lama ("The Dalai Lama and I know each other well"),[274] Louise David in fact met him only twice, which is certainly a better track record than that of her compatriot Henri d'Ollone, a military man trained at Saint-Cyr and an explorer, who was received on a single occasion by the 13th Dalai Lama during the latter's exile in China in 1908, but nothing compared to the longstanding friendship between Thubten Gyatso and Sir Charles Alfred Bell during the same period.

In 1912, the year of his meeting with "the first Buddhist in France," the Dalai Lama was in exile for a second time, this time in India, where he had established a close relationship with Charles Bell, the British district officer for Bhutan, Sikkim and Tibet. The two men had initially met on the Dalai Lama's arrival in Sikkim in 1912. Charles Bell, who was in charge of the latter's security and wellbeing, was passionately interested in Tibetan culture, spoke fluent Tibetan and was thus able to converse with the exiled sovereign in his own language. In his book, *Portrait of a Dalai Lama*,[275] Charles Bell discusses his friendship with the latter over 25 years. When the Dalai Lama was in Sikkim, he would visit him at least once a week and was received as an equal. The Dalai Lama would sit on a chair rather than a throne, forego blessing his guest, wear the white silk scarf around his wrist rather than his neck and had no need of an interpreter, bodyguards or chamberlains.

The two men conversed freely, essentially on political matters, but occasionally about religious questions, too.[276] Charles Bell always speaks of the 13th Dalai Lama with the greatest respect and admiration, often referring to him by using the literal English translation of Tibetan expressions (e.g., The Presence or the The Great Thirteenth), in sharp contrast to the pejorative terms such as the yellow Pope, the Tibetan Pope, the Lhasa Pontiff or the Deified Pontiff that abound in Louise David's writings.[277]

Actually, she considered the Dalai Lama virtually as an equal, a co-religionist who professed a number of original ideas without understanding Buddhism any better than herself. Thus, in her article for the *Mercure* she wrote: "What I had set out to do was not easy to accomplish. Up until the time I met him, the Dalai Lama had always categorically refused to receive European women. But I counted on the fact that he would give me an audience as a co-religionary for whom it was expected of him by leaders of the Buddhist faith to accord a cordial reception. For Buddhists the term co-religionary is vast and takes in people with markedly different opinions and beliefs – such was my own case in respect of the Lamaist Pope – and among Buddhists one prefers to fraternize rather than quibble over nebulous metaphysical questions which the Doctrinal Master, the Buddha himself forbade his followers from engaging in insofar as they did not lead to any practical or beneficial result."[278]

It was however on religious matters that Louise David wanted to converse with the Dalai Lama. In her article she is quite clear about her objectives: "I had gone to Kalimpong to talk with the Dalai Lama about the doctrines of his Church. I wished to speak to him not about the practices of the common people or superficial ritualism, of which those that have informed us about Lamaism have had some first-hand knowledge, but rather about the major philosophical theories (the fundamental tenets) of Buddhism, with the hope of ascertaining how much of them still informed the minds of educated Lamaists – and in particular that of the the Pontiff of Lhasa himself."[279]

Louise David thus remains faithful to her elitist conception of Buddhism, marked as it was by the greatest contempt for all forms of organized religious life.

As in the other Buddhist countries that she was familiar with, there existed in her opinion a clear difference between the great Aryan philosophy and popular superstition. To illustrate this point, she recounts the following incident: "An elderly lama of the Court in Lhasa arrived [this was while she was awaiting her second audience with the Dalai Lama], carrying two roughly wrapped parcels, one in a bath towel, the other in a piece of blue canvas. From them he took out two battered old books – Tibetan books made up of loose long narrow pages. He offered one to the Maharajah and then started to speak in the most garrulous fashion. All of a sudden, he turned towards me. We had met in Kalimpong and when I was about to leave, he had showered me with pious wishes.

"Once again, the miracle happened: the man was there, a talkative old soul, looking a trifle ridiculous with his towel spread over his knees and his tattered old books of magic spells (books of texts), but now it was no longer him that was speaking but the ancient wisdom of Indian thinkers which, in spite of superstition and ignorance, had taken root in the 'Land of Snows.' He went on uttering words, but did he understand what he was saying? Impossible to tell. And his wish for me was to make the Buddhas' dream come true – that of acquiring infinite wisdom, goodness without limit and a totally lucid view of Existence. I asked him, 'What is the way to salvation, the way to all-knowing wisdom?' He fixed his eyes on me for a brief moment and replied, 'You already know the answer, it lies in persevering thought, tireless meditation…' I know that he was right. His reply, which was strictly orthodox and faithful to a tradition far removed from the Lamaist Church, even ennobled him, and then his loquaciousness dried up… It was no more than a tiny spark. He got up and placed his rosary in the Maharajah's hands, which is a form of blessing and a wish for happiness."[280]

The "Great philosophy" only seems to be able to actualize itself in the minds of Tibetans in brief flashes and without their being aware of it. Only high-ranking lamas seem to be endowed with real intelligence. "I took pleasure in noticing, and take pleasure in saying it, that if the ordinary Tibetan in the street, like all ordinary people, is ignorant and superstitious, high-ranking Lamas such as the Dalai Lama certainly do not appear to be simpletons, or even savages, as people in Europe generally suppose them be."[281]

Nothing more is to be learned about Louise David's exchanges with the Dalai Lama, which did not develop in the way she had hoped they would: "Here I am before the Dalai Lama [for the second time, June 1912], for the last time in all probability, unless he manages to extricate himself from the current crisis and I am able visit him in his hometown, Lhasa. Our conversation was mainly about the manuscript that he had sent me and our future correspondence once he had returned to his capital, for he has very kindly expressed the wish to remain in contact with me and continue to help me with my research into contemporary northern Buddhist philosophy. No one has been more favored than I, and however great the distance that separates our way of thinking and the divergence between our opinions, I will always remember with gratitude the warm welcome that I received from the Tibetan Pope."[282]

However, on June 25, following her second meeting with the Dalai Lama, she wrote to her husband: "The fact of have continuing relations with a Dalai Lama is a chance of a lifetime which many an orientalist will envy me. That said, the man has little appeal for me beyond his being a brother in the cause of humanity. I dislike popes, I dislike the kind of Buddhist catholicism over which he presides. Everything about him is affected, he is lacking in both cordiality and genuine kindness."[283]

For the readership of the *Mercure de France* she paints a neutral portrait of this historical figure, being careful to avoid any kind of value judgement: "The Dalai Lama is thirty-seven years of age, so it is said, though he looks older. His official portrait, a photograph taken in Darjeeling and copiously reproduced, is not a good likeness. The 'touching-up' which photographers are so fond of doing gives him a blissful look, slightly sleepy, somewhat vacant, which is not at all how he really looks. The leader of the Lamaist Church is of medium height, of heavyish build, with a dark complexion but less so than that even of many Spaniards. His facial expression is determined, somewhat stubborn-looking."[284]

The rest of the description covers his psychology and the political circumstances behind his presence in Sikkim: "I have heard him be accused of cowardice because he has fled from Lhasa twice – first from the British, then from the Chinese. I know nothing of his deep feelings, but one should refrain from judging too rapidly a man who was brought up in the way Dalai Lamas are and living in the very special mental atmosphere that surrounds them. That he fled is the unavoidable truth of the matter. But why did he flee? That is what one needs to try and understand, but obviously it was impossible for me to put the question to him directly. He is said to be cruel in his politics, but are they really his or those of his ministers? And how odd it is that among those that prostrate themselves before him he is not always well liked. He does not come across as gloomy, and I saw him roar with laughter when I told him about the way the West judges the peoples of Asia. From the very outset, he showed himself to be ready and willing to help me with my research."[285]

In her article she says nothing about her work on lamaism, nor does she describe the religious practices of ordinary Tibetans, so it is necessary to refer to her letters for any genuine ethnological descriptions. From these letters much is to be learned about what she discovered on arriving in Sikkam in 1912. Her first experience of Tibetan Buddhism's ritual universe unfolded at the end of May. On May 28 she went to the monastery in Lachen, a neighboring village, accompanied by the Rev. Owen, a Tibetan-speaking British missionary who was to act as her interpreter. There she met the lama in charge of the monastery, Ngawang Kunzang Rinchen, lama nyingmapa, who was well-known in the region – and later among Western occult converts who were to follow in Louise David's footsteps.[286]

She describes the scene to her husband: "My dearest, just try to "realize" (as the English say) if you can the strangeness of the scene. We were in a lamaist oratory, and on the altar are Chenrési, Buddha and Padmasambhava, the great apostle of Tibet. On the walls there are frescos in which the symbolic Divinities in terrifying guise remind the initiates of the activity of existence, the destruction which produces life, and life coming into being only to be snatched away by Death. Grotesque-looking couples with skulls around their necks copulate with dead bodies under their feet – in short, all the ghastly symbology [sic] of tantrism which so fascinates Mr Woodroffe. Ancient banners hang down from the ceiling, two masques of devils decorate the stocky pillars painted in shocking red with Chinese-style capitals in blue and green. A small amount of light enters by the narrow window with colored glass. Amidst this decor, in the lotus position on a carpet, sits a strange and fascinating personage: the monastery of Lachen's father superior (gömpa), a man with an extraordinary reputation, a kind of 'Siddhipurusha,' half-magician, half-saint who for half the year lives outside the monastery, in solitude in a cave hidden behind a rock in some remote place, meditating alone as did the great legendary Yogis of the past. The local people consider him to be possessed with marvelous powers, including the ability to fly through space. He looks very different from the locals – a giant of a man, thin without being bony, with a plait of hair that comes down to his ankles.

"He was dressed in a red and yellow Tibetan costume quite different from those worn by the lamas in Sikkim. He has an extremely intelligent face, bold, decided, lit up by extraordinary eyes – eyes from whose depths a dazzling light seems to shoot up, the sign of intense yogic (spiritual) practice… But there was also much more than mere intellectual satisfaction in the hour that I spent there. There was something awesome, grandiose, immensely impressive in the way that the yogi with a great sweeping movement of his arm dismissed the panoply of surrounding images and symbols: 'They are only good for the simple-minded' and, paraphrasing the Upanishad, India's chief source of wisdom: find all in thyself."[287]

The main hypothesis on which Louise David's new work on Tibetan Buddhism was based was that that northern Buddhism had been penetrated by Vedanta philosophy. It was this possible connection that she wanted to investigate by exchanging with the high-ranking lamas such as the the father superior of Lachen monastery and the 13th Dalai Lama.[288]

On May 30 in Lachen she had her first opportunity to attend Tantric ceremonies – as an invited master: "My young friend (virtually a disciple) [The maharajah Sidkéong Tulku Namgyal] and I set out to climb the steep slope leading to Gömpa. As soon as we had left the bungalow, the lama musicians, lined up along the edge of the monastery's parapet wall and began to play, while a crowd of hangers-on of various kinds dressed in curious attire followed us at a respectful distance, and a sort of bodyguard walked in front of us leading the procession. People would appear suddenly along the way, prostrating themselves flat out in the Chinese fashion. I acknowledged these prostrations since I was walking ahead of the prince. At the entrance to the monastery we were welcomed by all the red lamas headed by the Great Lama Superior. The musicians, the bearers of parasols, banners, etc., formed a thick wall. Several of them were blowing into Tibetan trumpets which are so long that the end rests on the ground. It was extraordinarily picturesque. We were on a sort of terrace that looked out over the valley and I had the impression of being on a theatre stage.

"Unfortunately, it was drizzling with rain but, come what may, I had to have a photograph as a souvenir, however drab it might turn out. The Maharajah, himself a photographer, advised me to use an extra-long exposure, given the lack of light, but was this good advice? In our beige waterproofs we looked like two news reporters in the midst of the multicolored crowd. Once we had taken the photographs we headed for the monastery. We took off our coats and went into the sanctuary. The prince bowed three times, a little embarrassed by my presence. He was aware of my opinions concerning ceremonies of this kind. For my part, I simply honored the Hindu Saint Chenrési-Avalokiteçwara, who is the symbol of the most beautiful Oriental ideal, with an ordinary salutation.

"Then the lamas sang the 'three refuge' verses in Tibetan, which with a choir sounded quite different from the way they are recited in Ceylon. A dish of rice was brought to the Maharajah, who with a wave of the hand indicated that it be passed to me. All this was pure ritual… Finally, just for the sake of the exotic and to rise to the occasion, I decided to take the plunge: I picked up a few grains of rice and tried to remember the appropriate 'mudra' along with the correct finger position to adopt. Of course, my knowledge of what to do was based purely on what I had learnt during my academic studies. I thought I was now just about in the right position… fortunately it was dark in the temple! At last, the ceremony was over, and it was time to throw one's grains of rice towards the altar. I managed to remember that much and throw my rice in the correct manner, as the prince had done, the others in attendance waiting for me to finish before throwing their own. Amen, the ritual was finally over!

"The Maharajah was now to sit on a sort of small pontifical throne to the left of the altar, and opposite him a seat covered by a carpet had been prepared for me. If only you could have seen me! … The lamas remained lining the walls, not being allowed to sit down in the presence of the prince-pontiff. As soon as we were seated, the whole assembly bowed profusely. The Maharajah then gave a speech, a summary of which he translated for me, and in turn I spoke, with him translating. Oh! those speeches made in exotic places, amidst strange idols, alarming symbols, and the fantastic audience of red lamas … how often they come to mind when I am lecturing in Europe. Then the monastery's Superior [of Lachen, met two days earlier] after taking off his mitre walked over to position himself in the central nave. He bowed to the prince and then with a scarf in his clasped hands, proceeded to speak interminably before his great leader in a voice trembling with emotion. In this emotional state and display of humility he looked far less of a philosopher than he had the day before. The speech was long, very long, indeterminable, punctuated by frequent bows – so frequent in fact that several times the prince had to curtail them with a wave of his hand. I was far from bored, however, and watched the spectacle with the utmost relish. Finally, it was over, and I got up from my episcopal seat."[289]

A little later, just as they were about to have tea with a group of dignitaries, she had no qualms about sermonizing the ascetic: "Then, as I had a dressing-down in mind for this longhaired hermit, I got up from my seat, which I disliked, returned to the bench in the tantric oratory where I had sat a couple of days before, and launched into a speech about the great doctrine that the lamaists had forgotten or kept selfishly for themselves, leaving ordinary people prey to primitive superstition. The prince, who was most impressed, acted as interpreter. Had the longhaired ascetic understood that there was no salvation in selfishness and that the 'ivory tower' in which thinkers who ignore the mental strife of others live is a tower of perdition? My young friend told me that the words of a foreigner would have a greater effect on him than his own and that he thought that the hermit had got the message. And on that note the session was closed."[290]

It was not just the links between Vedanta and northern Buddhism that Lousie David wanted to fathom, nor did she want to become famous as a European orientalist solely by virtue of her ethnographic prowess. She hoped also to reform Tibetan Buddhism, that is, to lead it back to its roots in the reputedly pure tradition of Indian Buddhism, which was supposedly free of rites and customs. She was assisted in this undertaking by Sidkéong Tulku Namgyal, the son of the Maharajah of Sikkim, heir to the throne and the father superior of a monastery in the region. Louise David had met Sidkéong Tulku on arriving in Kalimpong in April 1912. The Maharajah's son, who had been educated in a British college in Darjeeling and then at Oxford, was an anglophile, and it was through her frequentation of English circles that she first met him staying in a bungalow that was used by British officials and explorers: "The Maharajah had arrived a short time before me at the bungalow. He immediately sent me his card and I went to see him. A whole side of the building had been reserved for him. The Maharajah Kumar (heir to the throne) is the son of the reigning Maharajah. He is a very friendly young man who appears to be highly intelligent. He was magnificently dressed in gold brocade."[291]

They conversed about Buddhism, about which they shared a modernist – i.e., secularist – conception. Following the advice of Louise David, the young man in fact became an enthusiastic Freemason soon afterwards. After her meeting with the Dalai Lama, she compared the two men, praising the young Maharajah's son, whom she found similar to "the contemporary Buddhist writers" that she had praised in her article of 1909.

On April 15 she wrote: "On getting back to my bungalow, I met up again with the amiable young Maharadjah Kumar. He is considerably more intelligent than the Dalai Lama and he is full of good intent as regards making a useful contribution in his tiny state. Poor little heir to the throne with clipped wings… He has been to Paris and Peking, seen the whole of Europe, and studied at an English university. Even if he does wear a costume of the same cut and color as that worn by the Pope of Lhasa, his mentality is quite different, and we are able to speak almost as friends. 'Ah! If only I were the Dalai Lama,' he said to me, 'if only I had the power to reform Tibetan Buddhism!' I replied to him jokingly, 'If you were the Dalai Lama you wouldn't think the way you do think. You would neither have travelled, nor seen the world, nor studied as you have done, and you'd be just like he is.' We chatted about our shared acquaintances and friends…"

Louise David and Sidkéong Tulku became friends. Older than him and carrying the natural authority attached to being European when it came to advanced ideas, she became his advisor – not only in religious matters but personal ones too, even advising him on his marriage plans. They met regularly to discuss a hypothetical reform of Tibetan Buddhism in which she believed she could play an important role. On May 30, 1912 she wrote: "In the evening, as it was the day of the full moon, the monthly Sunday festival for

Buddhists, we performed our devotions together, that is to say, we read the Dhammapada and discussed philosophical questions. We came up with various useful reforms regarding the lamas, religious education, etc. I dare to hope that my visit to the country will have had left some mark on the social development and education of the people."[292] In May, when her plans for reform with Sidkéong Tulku were in full swing, she wrote a *Brochure, à l'usage des bouddhistes*, which she had translated into Tibetan with the aim of inciting the local population to change their ways.[293]

A letter dating from June 1912 shows her adopting an ambivalent line vis à vis Tibetan clerics, whom she considered worthy of respect only insofar as they accepted to be sermonized by her: "Concerning sermons, I am to give one, in grand style in Gangtok in the monastery temple for the young lamas who are there for their higher education studies in Tibetan language and religious philosophy. The Maharaja Kumar will attend along with all the educated people of Gangtok. Naturally, I will have an interpreter who will repeat in Tibetan what I say. This will take place after a lamaist ceremony on the day of the full moon, in six days, on the 29th… Of course, I will be the first European ever to preach in such a place. Lamaists are often criticized, and deservedly so given their ignorance, but do they not at the same time demonstrate a certain broad-mindedness in inviting someone such as myself – with convictions so different from theirs and with my hostility to their superstitions?"[294]

In April 1912 she made the acquaintance of an important figure in the history of Tibetan Buddhism's dissemination in the West, the person who served as interpreter to her for just this kind of lecture – Kazi Dawa Samdup. The principal of a school in Gantok, he worked as an interpreter for the British and Tibetan governments as well as a resource for Western Theosophers. In addition to Louise David, to whom he gave Tibetan lessons and whom he accompanied during her official appointments, notably with the Dalai Lama, Kazi Dawa

Samdup also knew John Woodroffe and in 1919 translated into English a selection of Tibetan texts for the American Theosopher, Walter Evans-Wentz. Once translated and preceded by an imposing introduction by Evans-Wentz these texts were to form the basis of the famous *Tibetan Book of the Dead* (1921), a work that was unknown even to the Tibetans themselves.[295]

The first time she mentions him, in a letter to her husband, she presents him as a man of letters: "He [Sidkéong Tulku] has very kindly brought me from Gangtok, the college principal, a man of letters who had very interesting things to say and has passed on to me some of his work. He has written a biography about a delightful Tibetan poet by the name of Milarepa."[296] Here and there in her letters she briefly mentions him, but it is in one of her most popular books on Tibet that she paints the most striking portrait of him, one that stands in total contrast with the reverential and enigmatic way in which Evans-Wentz speaks of him in the *Tibetan Book of the Dead*.

Here is what she has to say about Kazi Dawa Samdup in *With Mystics and Magicians in Tibet*,[297] a book written in a strongly Theosophical vein: "Dawasandup was very interested in all things relating to the death and the afterlife of a 'spirit.' Five or six years after having personally explained to me his ideas on the subject, he translated a classic work from the Tibetan on the wanderings of the deceased in the afterlife [*The Tibetan Book of the Dead*, co-authored by Evans-Wentz]. Several foreigners – British officials and orientalists – used Dawasandup's services and recognized his talent. Nonetheless, I have every reason to believe that they were not aware of his true, very colorful personality, which he was very careful to hide. Dawasandup was an occultist and in a certain way might even qualify as a mystic. He went in search of secret communion with the Dakinis and the fearsome deities; he was immensely attracted by anything to do with the mysterious world of invisible beings. He also had something of a gift for mediumship, which the necessity to work to earn a living prevented him from cultivating to the extent that he would have liked…"

Discreet as he was in his occultist activities, Dawasandup was also, according to Louise David, somewhat weak morally, notably when it came to alcohol: "Although Dawasandup admired the irreproachable morality of this holy lama [his guru], such heights of perfection seemed to be so far beyond him that there was no point in trying to attain them – this he humbly confessed. What attracted him beyond all else, as I have already said, was contact with beings of the occult world with a view to acquiring paranormal powers. To witness supernatural phenomena (miracles), to be able to produce them himself, such was his dream. He was fired by the aspirations of a magician without possessing the necessary learning or moral strength to reach his goal – this he humbly admitted. A penchant for alcohol, all too frequent among his compatriots, was the bane of his existence. It brought out in him a natural predisposition to anger which on one occasion led him to within a hair's breadth of committing murder."

She went on to pride herself on having had "some influence over him for as long as she was staying in Gangtok," having got him to stop drinking to obey Buddhist precepts. She noted also that he was a severe and violent schoolmaster who did not refrain from hitting his pupils.[298]

A fourth personality emerges in Louise David's writings about Sikkim, in addition to the modern-thinking son of the Maharajah of Sikkim, the 13th Dalai Lama (immersed in pomp and ceremony and superstition), and the interpreter and alcoholic occultist Tibetan teacher. This is Ngawang Kunzang Rinchen, the famous "long-haired ascetic (hermit)" whom she refers to as the "gomchen [father superior] of Lachen monastery." Clearly this practicing tantrist had initially left her with mixed feelings – on the positive side, he agreed with her views on "the great Indian philosophy." On the downside, he was wont to excessive bowing at the slightest provocation whenever in the presence of anyone more powerful.

It was nonetheless under his supervision that from October 1914 to September 1916 she was able to experience the life of a hermit living in retreat in a cave – with several lengthy breaks, notably in July and August 1916 when she travelled to Tibet. The idea was first put to her in the autumn of 1914, when she was still endeavoring to complete her reform projects with the son of the maharajah. On March 18 she wrote to her husband: "The lamas want to build a hut for me on one of the neighboring mountain tops so that I can go and stay there when the urge takes me. It is the custom here – more so perhaps than in India – for religious people of importance to go into retreat on some steep slope. I had absolutely nothing against following this custom but, to tell the truth, my dreams were less ambitious. I thought simply of having a small shelter close to Gömba, a sort of 'sanctuary' providing the end point of a long walk and a place where I could go and sit in the afternoon with my books.

"The trusty lamas did not for one moment suspect the tameness of my idea, and straight away started pointing at mountain peaks lost in the clouds which they thought would be worthy of me, so that I did not even have the opportunity to express my ridiculously bourgeois and prosaic original idea."[299]

So, the religious retreat was not Louise David's own initiative but rather a consequence of the level of misunderstanding (and perhaps wariness) that persisted between her and the lamas. Taking her to be a practicing Buddhist, they sought to provide her with the means to develop her asceticism. It was also, as she pointed out, a ploy for testing the foreigner that she was: "Good souls... but perhaps a little skeptical about the European lady who grants herself the right to wear sacred 'gömpchen' rings – albeit legitimately, since she was given them by a famous gömpchen. They want to see if this Western lady is not merely a papier mâché gömpchen and whether she is capable of following the custom."[300]

In a light-hearted spirit she accepted what had befallen her: "What a strange turn to my life, going to spend weeks if not months or (even) years, as some do, all alone, with no other soul at hand, with no other human presence in proximity, except for the peasant who every three or four days, drops by with water. When one is a Tibetan, one makes one's tea by oneself, mixes in barley flour, eats cheese and soup made with dried meat – but when one is a Western hermit one takes along a few cans of food. It is a sort of game – a game which is not to everyone's taste, and I know what I am talking about, for many are those who would hardly relish those lonely nights spent in the jungle in a flimsy hut of plaited bamboo."[301] It was therefore not because she wanted to become a Buddhist in the Tibetan style that Louise David undertook the retreat, but because chance circumstances gave her the opportunity, which she seized with her natural love of a challenge.

It is difficult to ascertain the true nature of Louise David's retreat experience. In theory, if he had considered her a genuine disciple (which is still unproven) and if the gömchen had checked that the long and painstaking preliminary exercises (*ngöntro*) common to all schools of tantric Buddhism had been completed – which obviously was not the case, given her distaste for ritual practices – he would have subsequently revealed to her the highest teachings of the Nyingma school. This would involve reading and commenting on *dzogchen* (Great Perfection) texts and by having her do eye exercises – pressing her eyeballs and staring at the sky, into a mirror and into total darkness.[302] In fact, she says nothing about the private initiation she underwent, either in her letters or in her books about tantric doctrines and religious practices written later. To her husband she speaks mainly about daily life, the village festivities she took part in, difficulties in obtaining food and fuel for heating, and about her health problems.

She also speaks of the virtues of spartan living, shares with him her pessimistic views on the war raging in Europe, and rejects his divorce proposal. At no time does she reveal what the gömchen had taught her – something that was probably of no interest to Philippe Néel. She mentions, however, that they had agreed she teach him English in exchange for Tibetan lessons and in addition – so she hoped – a presentation of some of the "mysteries of tantric Buddhism which were totally unknown to orientalists."[303] In September 1914 she wrote that the fundamental objective of the retreat was "a collaborative book, a comparative study of lamaism and Vedanta that I am writing," which is reminiscent of Evans Wentz and Kazi Dawa Samdup's collaboration on the *The Tibetan Book of the Dead*. In short, she had no personal expectations of a mystical kind but rather was motivated by objectives that were purely linguistic and editorial in nature.

In her two great books on Tibetan spiritual practices, *With Mystics and Magicians in Tibet* (1929) and *Initiations and Initiates in Tibet* (1930), the fruit of her extensive visits with Tibetan clerics, and in particular the lama of Lachen, the only reference to *dzogchen* appears in a single footnote.[304] She does not try to present a comprehensive study of this particular school, as specialists of today would be inclined to do, but rather she describes several of its main practices, with the lama of Lachen in all likelihood her main source of information. In the central chapter of *Initiations and Initiates in Tibet* entitled "Daily Spiritual Exercises,"[305] a description is given of typical *dzogchen* visualization exercises such as imagining "one's body to be like a mountain," "one's eyes to be like an ocean" or "one's mind to be like the sky."[306] The fact that she describes in detail the color and light visualization exercises of the vowel A and "dream yoga" – both well-known today – also suggests that she had first-hand experience of these techniques and was almost certainly one of the first Europeans to practice them. But what kind of a practitioner was she?

To answer this question, it is necessary to look through her writings for the occasional passages where she mentions, though never very clearly, what her exact position was vis-à-vis Lamaist spiritual practices. On this point, a passage in *With Mystics and Magicians in Tibet* is particularly interesting: "The Tibetans had accepted me as a lady-lama. They knew that I was a Buddhist but were unable to comprehend the difference between my purely philosophic conception of Buddhism and the lamaist variety. Thus, in order to have the trust and confidence that went with the religious attire that I wore [and she adds in a footnote: "Being moreover legitimately entitled to wearing it – I would never have dreamed of using it as a mere disguise."], I was obliged to observe Tibetan customs, and in particular religious customs. This requirement constituted a serious obstacle to certain scientific observations that I could have made, but it was the price I had to pay to gain access to a domain that was considerably more jealously guarded than Tibetan territory."[307]

It is generally acknowledged by Tibetologists that her presentation of *mahayana* religious practices is in the main exact and precise. That said, these two books – in particular, *With Mystics and Magicians in Tibet* – are strongly influenced by theosophy and as a result have been somewhat marginalized by specialists in the field. They follow the same format as *L'Inde où j'ai vécu* with few or no references at all to the contemporary literature on the subject. The chapters are well organized but marred by numerous digressions and anecdotes, personal memories, and unexpected tangents. The book mainly focuses on the master-disciple relationship, the initiation processes, and "psychic phenomena," which the author attempts to explain scientifically, notably with reference to her personal experiences.

For example, in her letters and in a chapter of *With Mystics and Magicians in Tibet* devoted to "psychic sports"[308] she mentions personal experimentation with *tummo*, the "yoga of inner heat" that enables some ascetics to not feel the cold. She confesses to her husband her desire "to cut herself off up there to try out certain lamaist theories concerning heat generation. They themselves endlessly discuss this subject in writing and amongst themselves, certain hermits living naked in the snows – I have always been curious about curious things."[309] Another of these psychic sports is what the Tibetans call *loung gom*, which she defines as "a kind of exercise that is half psychic, half physical, aimed at enabling one to acquire supernormal lightness and speed." The progressive acquisition of the ability "to run considerable distances at great speed without food or rest," levitation, the generation of inner heat (*tummo*) and telepathy figure among the phenomena she describes and attempts to demystify using materialist explanations – while denouncing what she calls "imposters."[310] She herself was convinced that the *tummo* technique really did work, since she had seen with her own eyes how ascetics were able to live completely naked at very high altitudes.[311] She also adds: "Speaking personally, my limited experiments with *toumo* led me to obtain some interesting results."[312]

It was not as a convert to Tibetan Buddhism that Louise David practiced these different kinds of rituals but as an occultist, albeit a disillusioned one – in contrast to her contemporary, Woodroffe. She wanted above all to experiment scientifically with the Tibetans' spiritual techniques to reveal how they worked without recourse to any form of transcendence. In that she was a precursor of the "scientific Buddhism" of the late 20th and early 21st centuries, which occupies a preeminent place in the neurological study of meditative states.[313] For her, "spiritual" has more to do with a cerebral function rather than a sphere of animate activity disconnected from matter. It is in this way that she interprets *cittamatra* ("all is mind"), the lama of Lachen's philosophical doctrine – a form of non-materialist idealism which views all physical phenomena as being of the same nature as the mind rather than being a purely mental projection without a basis in reality, as she would have it.

When she writes to her husband, using a well-known Buddhist metaphor according to which "human-beings are like wrecked ships floating at the mercy of the waves on a havenless sea,"[314] she is being only partially Buddhist. A true Buddhist would say, depending on the particular school, either that havens do exist and that Buddha leads the way to them, or alternatively that the illusion of the need to find a haven will eventually disappear, so it is important not to lose hope or energy.

Also, when she writes that life is "a theatre of poor bewitched puppets possessed by a constant state of striving before briefly exhausting themselves and then falling out of existence," she is not being entirely faithful to what she was taught by her lama. For him, human beings are mostly "bewitched puppets," "products of multiple causes and, as such, not free in their actions and hardly aware of the nature of the strings that move them."[315] But after their physical death they are destined to be reborn so that one day they can attain the state of Liberation.

The lama of Lachen believed that consciousness is not tied to the body and that it survives in one form or another after death. He believed that the lives of all beings are destined to end in happiness. The Buddhas and the Bodhisattvas intervene in the six realms (during the cycle of existence) specifically to lead them to this goal. He believed in the effectiveness of rituals, in gods, hells and paradises. In short, he could not be considered a follower of Nietzsche or Schopenhauer or Stirner, despite his unorthodox Parisian disciple's opinion on the matter.

A letter that was recently rediscovered in an old trunk full of stage costumes clearly shows the extent of the misunderstanding that existed between Louise David and the lama of Lachen.[316] In it she states – in English – that she is a disciple of Buddha, that she is both happy and honored to be counted among his disciples, that her interest in Buddhism goes beyond that of a "university professor" and is informed by a genuine personal religious and philosophical conviction, and that her aim is to spread Buddhism in her own country.

But immediately afterwards, adopting a more independent stance, she adds that she does not believe in rebirth, in heavens or hells, nor in the utility of ritual, which she compares to childish games. It is quite likely that the lama never read this letter, so we shall never know what he would have made of it. What we do know, thanks to the German convert to Buddhism Anagarika Govinda (Ernst Lothar Hoffman) who followed in Louise David's footsteps in the 1930s, is that the Father Superior of the monastery in Lachen clearly intended to make use of the strange Parisian lady-Buddhist to disseminate Tibetan religious practices in the West.[317]

Having definitively conjoined the ideas that life is nothing but a dream and the world nothing more than a stage, she thus discovered quite by chance – without any personal calling apart from being attracted by the landscape and the way of life – a new theatre to explore, the world of Tibet, in which she voluntarily became a new heroine.

After her unplanned yet all-important stay in Sikkim, Louise David decided to explore the regions to the west of Tibet in order to acquaint herself with their varied landscapes, customs and religious beliefs. Her objective was as much personal (the pleasure of discovering new places on foot) as professional (the desire to write about a world that was still barely known at the time). She made a first clandestine excursion to Shigatzé in July 1916 during which she met other important lamas, such as the Tashi lama, but was subsequently expelled from Sikkim by the British authorities precisely because of these escapades. She then went on to Japan, a country which she did not much like and where she stayed for about six months. She next travelled through Korea and parts of China, spending the winter of 1917-1918 in Peking (embroiled in civil war at the time), and then returned to Tibet. She stayed for two and a half years at the monastery in Kumbun and explored the region. The excursions she made from there provided material for her book, *Au pays des brigands gentilshommes* (1933). She also had the opportunity to hear bards recount the legend of the Tibetan hero Guésar, which gave rise to another book, *La Vie surhumaine de Guésar de Ling* (1931), which was prefaced by the celebrated Indologist Sylvain Lévi.

Finally, she was to set out on her famous expedition to Lhasa in the company of one of her young servants, the devoted and resourceful Aphur Yongden who, under the name of Albert, later became her adopted son. After several unsuccessful attempts, the journalist and one-time Parisian opera singer, then 56 years old, disguised herself as a Tibetan beggar and with Aphur Yongden managed to slip into a crowd of pilgrims heading towards Lhasa for the Mönam festival (Festival of the Great Prayer).

They stayed in the Tibetan capital for two months, visiting temples and monasteries without being received by any Tibetan dignitaries – doubtless because they sought to remain anonymous. This expedition was an outstanding physical and mental feat, for they had to find their way across unknown territory and endure considerable hardship, such as intense cold and a cruel lack of food. She tells the story of this journey in her first successful book, *My Journey to Lhasa* (1927).[318] Louise David had at last undergone her true initiation. She had become the great female explorer, Alexandra David-Néel, and had finally gained recognition as a great writer. She had succeeded in entering history – through the gates of Lhasa.

After her successful and exhausting expedition to Lhasa she returned to India and then to France, where she settled in the small Provençal town of Digne-les-Bains. There she dedicated her life to writing. She also organized many conferences in Paris and other European cities, taking with her lama Yongden, a precious indigenous specimen from Tibet. From 1937 to 1946 she and Yongden began a second, long journey from Brussels to China, the Tibetan Marches and India, passing through Moscow aboard the Trans-Siberian. There she discovered new political realities that left their mark on her work: the application of communism in Russia and China, which she described in her book *Sous des nuées d'orage* (Under stormy clouds); the war with Japan; the revolt of the Tibetans in the regions of Kham and Amdo (a conflict between two models of society, which she writes of in *Le vieux Tibet face à la Chine nouvelle*, Old Tibet faces New China); and finally the struggle for independence in India, which is largely echoed in *L'Inde où j'ai vécu* (India where I lived).

After this second Asian tour, aged 78, she returned to France and produced other books, mostly dedicated to Tibetan religions and Indian philosophies. She died at age 101, with an unfinished book on her desk, *Rencontre de désincarnés* (Encounters of the Disembodied), about the similarities between the ancient Chinese philosophers she studied in her youth and the new Maoist thinkers.

She became a legend in the realm of Eastern spirituality and attracted many pilgrims to her house. She was read by several generations of artists, among whom featured the Beat poets in America and Hergé, the creator of Tintin, in Belgium.

7

From Modern to Materialistic Buddhism

Louise David spent her long life building a unique destiny as a peerless, real-life pathfinder and an icon of spiritual freedom. On her journey she also shared in the invention and promotion of a specific trend of modern Buddhism. Known as materialistic Buddhism, it is a tradition that takes the Buddha as its founder while infusing the trend with 19th-century positivist ideas.

Indeed, the doctrine she created under the name of Buddhism is the hybrid product of her own intellectual career. It is, in a sense, the result of her personal fall – from the realm of the spiritual to the pure material. Abandoning any belief in a personal God, full of mysteries and capable of miracles, then favoring an abstract pantheistic and rational faith, she ended up embracing nihilism.

Louise David not only lost her faith in God and his meaningful creations during her intellectual journey – she also lost all faith in human beings and in all forms of non-materialistic life. Life to her had no explanation and no reason, and it stopped at death. There is no eternal life and no resurrection, nor any kind of rebirth or enlightenment. There is nothing. And since there is nothing beyond, there is also nothing inside. In the heart of matter, there is no spirit. There is only matter. What we call the spirit, or the spiritual, is a mere illusion, a strange and unexpected product of the brain cells. Therefore, all religions, including the Asian Buddhist traditions, are but human inventions. They should be deconstructed and denounced as mere tools of oppression. On her descent from the heights of faith, Louise David brought modern Buddhism with her and imbued it with a new strain of antispirituality.

She may have claimed to be a Buddhist but, seeing the world through a nihilistic lens, she also defined her own Buddhist tradition as a materialistic doctrine in which metaphysics, ethics, rituals, and other social practices, so beloved by Asian practitioners, counted for nothing. What counted for her was how certain simple ideas, such as the Four Noble Truths, could help relieve suffering in a rational or, as she put it, in an "arithmetic" way. It is clear from her writings that by rational she mostly meant "mental." She thought relief from suffering is essentially an event that happens in one's head. It is nothing more than a change of perspective: one should *decide to think* of one's suffering – and indeed of one's entire life – as a complete illusion. This is an act of will and requires an effort of insight.

This could be seen as authentically Buddhist, except for the fact that she did not believe in an afterlife. Her sombre stoicism was only concerned with today, perhaps tomorrow, but never with the day after she dies – because thinking stops at the moment of death, and after she stops thinking she stops living – so why bother? That she understood "rationality" and its by-product "modernity" as mere synonyms of cold logic and "cognitivity" is also confirmed by the fact that she never undertook any charitable work. She had absolutely no interest in relieving suffering in the most human, concrete way. In any case, she never wrote that she did, or that she should, or that anyone ever ought to. Her "Buddhist" fight against suffering was either purely theoretical or simply self-centered.

To be fair, however, it is notable that she adopted her young Tibetan servant Yongden, taking him with her to Europe, offering him French nationality, shelter, food, and recognition for the rest of his short life (he died in 1955, fourteen years before her). This is certainly proof of compassion and emotional attachment, but in general she remained a solitary, detached thinker.

She may have seen Buddhism as a remedy, a soteriology, a terrestrial salvation path. She may have spent her life elaborating it carefully, as one carves a statue, but she never seemed to be really interested in its implementation or dissemination in any *practical* form. She gave conferences, she wrote books, but she never wished to teach anything she learned in Tibet. She never became a master. This is perhaps the most striking feature of her Buddhist modernity. She was and remained the intellectual – closer to Madame Blavatsky than to Annie Besant.

If she never taught nor even practiced Buddhism as Westerners do today, it is for one simple reason, as shown in these pages – she despised rituals and other socio-religious events. What interested her was exposing rituals as basically a neurological phenomenon, and that was all there was to say about them. To her, all human phenomena can be reduced to biological events, and reality is only biology. The meaning and function of Buddhist rituals had to be found in the brain, and nowhere else. This attitude may be regarded as modern, but it should be more rightly called materialistic. Indeed, how it differs from the centuries-long Asian traditions is above all the fact that Materialistic Buddhism focuses on the brain and its unknown functions – a typical 19th-century occultist obsession – based on the implicit premise that the mind, or spirit, is nothing more than a chemical product of some sophisticated human cells.

This way of viewing Buddhist rituals, so characteristic of Louise David, strangely reminds us of what this ancient Asian religion has become for many practitioners and thinkers today: a powerful science of the mind whose efficacity can supposedly be proven in high-tech laboratories, and from which will surely result emotional happiness and physical well-being, rather than a way out of this world.

Does this mean that the Parisian Buddhist Louise David was responsible for the disappearance of metaphysics and ethics in modern Buddhism and for its reduction to some kind of nihilistic, hedonistic, solitary practice? She certainly was not the only one, but she did play an important part in the process, for she had many readers. In a way, she summarized in her own self the evolution and transformation of Buddhism as it was imported into the West: an exotic type of esotericism turned clinical.

Chronology

1868 Louise Eugénie Alexandrine Marie David is born in Saint-Mandé, Paris, on October 24. Spends her childhood in Paris, Bléré in the Tours region, and Brussels.

1871 Her father brings her to the Communards' Wall.

1880 Enters a Catholic boarding school.

1886 Starts studying at the Royal Conservatory of Brussels.

1889 Obtains a First Prize in singing (*chant théâtral français*), visits Brussels Carmel.

1890 Starts her singing tours in Belgium and France.

1892 Travels to England. Becomes a member of the Theosophical Society.

1893 Joins anarchist groups and is initiated to Freemasonry.

1894-6 Travels to Ceylon, India and Indochina.

1896 Returns to Paris, rue Nicolo (Passy).

1897-9 Sings in various theaters in France and Belgium.

1900 Starts a singing tour of Greece, France, and Tunisia. Meets Philippe Néel. Takes several excursions, notably to North Africa and Switzerland. Publishes her first book, *Pour la vie*.

1902 Becomes artistic director of the Casino of Tunis.

1903 Visits Spain. Gives lectures in Paris. Starts her journalistic collaboration with *La Fronde*.

1904 Marries Philippe Néel. Travels in France, Belgium, England, Italy, North Africa.

1905 Takes part in the Free Thought Congress in Paris and in meetings of the *Société d'Anthropologie*.

1906 Travels in North Africa, Belgium and England.

1907 Stays in Tunisia, France, and Switzerland. Publishes her first scholarly book, *Le philosophe Meh-ti (ou Mo-tse) et l'Idée de solidarité*.

1908 Travels to Italy and participates in the congress of the Italian Women's association in Rome. Stays in England.

1909 Gives several lectures in Paris, notably at the Grand Orient de France.

1910 Stays in England and Scotland. Gives her first courses on Buddhism at the Université nouvelle in Brussels.

1911 Publishes *Le modernisme bouddhiste* et *Le bouddhisme du Bouddha*. Attends masonic lodges and meetings of the Société anthropologique. Travels to Northern Africa. Sails to India. Arrives in Ceylon.

1912 Arrives and settles in Calcutta. Has an audience with the 13th Dalai Lama in Sikkim.

1913 Travels to Nepal and returns to Sikkim.

1914-16 On a retreat under the direction of the Gomchen of Lachen.

1916 Travels secretly to Shigatze and is expelled from Sikkim.

1916-17 Sails to Japan.

1917 Stays in Korea.

1917-18 Spends the winter in Peking.

1918-21 Stays at Kumbum Monastery.

1921-22 Stays at Jyekundo.

1923-24 Expedition to Lhasa, dressed as a beggar.

1924-25 Returns to India.

1925 Returns to France.

1928 Settles in Digne-les-Bains, Southern France.

1925-37 Travels in France, Italy, Switzerland, Belgium, Holland, Germany, Eastern Europe, Northern Africa. Gives numerous conferences.

1937-46 Travels to China.

1946-69 Resident in Digne-les-Bains. Dies at almost 101 years old on September 8, 1969.

Bibliography

Books by Alexandra David-Néel

Pour la vie, réflexions sur tous les faits de société. Brussels, 1900. Reedited in *Féministe et libertaire, Ecrits de jeunesse.* Paris, Éditions Les nuits rouges, 2013.

Le philosophe Meh-ti (ou Mo-tse) et l'Idée de solidarité. Luzac et Cie, London, 1907. Reedited in *En Chine.* Paris, Plon, 1970.

Les Théories individualistes dans la philosophie chinoise. Giard et Brière, Paris, 1909. Reedited in *En Chine.* Paris, Plon, 1970.

Le féminisme rationnel. Paris, 1909. Reedited in *Féministe et libertaire, Ecrits de jeunesse.* Paris, Éditions Les nuits rouges, 2013.

Le Modernisme bouddhiste et le bouddhisme du Bouddha, Paris, Alcan, 1911; Revised version: *Le bouddhisme du Bouddha*, Paris, Editions du Rocher, 1921. New edition: *Le bouddhisme du Bouddha*, Paris, Editions du Rocher, 1977.

Voyage d'une Parisienne à Lhasa. Paris, Plon, 1927. American edition: *My Journey to Lhasa.* Harper and Brothers, New York, 1927. Reprint: Beacon Press, Boston, 1986.

Mystiques et magiciens du Tibet. Paris, Plon, 1929. American edition: *Magic and Mystery in Tibet*, 1929. Reprint: Dover, New York, 1971.

Initiations lamaïques. Paris, Adyar, 1930. American edition: *Initiations and Initiates in Tibet*, 1930.

Avec la collaboration du Lama Yongden, *La Vie surhumaine de Guésar de Ling: L'Iliade des Tibétains.* Paris, Editions du Rocher, 1931. American edition: *The Superhuman Life of Gesar of Ling*, 1934.

Au pays des brigands gentilshommes. Paris, Plon, 1933.

Le lama aux cinq sagesses, roman tibétain. Paris, Plon, 1935.

Magie d'amour et magie noire: Scènes du Tibet Inconnu. Paris, Plon, 1938. American edition, *Tibetan Tale of Love and Magic.*

Le bouddhisme: ses doctrines, ses méthodes. Paris, Editions du Rocher, 1939.

Au cœur des Himalayas. Le Népal. Paris, Pygmalion, 1949.

L'Inde. Hier-aujourd'hui-demain. Paris, Plon, 1951.

Astavakra Gitâ. Discours sur le Vedânta advaita (translation from the Sanskrit). Paris, Adyar, 1951.

Textes tibétains inédits, translated and presented by Alexandra David-Néel, Paris, La Colombe, 1952. Re-edition: Paris, Pygmalion, 1977.

Les enseignements secrets des bouddhistes tibétains. La vue pénétrante, Paris, Pygmalion, 1951. New edition: Paris, Adyar, 1961.

Le Vieux Tibet face à la Chine nouvelle. Paris, Plon, 1953.

La Puissance du Néant. Paris, Plon, 1954.

La Connaissance transcendante d'après le texte et les commentaires tibétains. Paris, Adyar, 1958.

Avadhûtâ Gîtâ de Dattatraya. Poème mystique Vedânta advaita. Paris, Adyar, 1958.

Le Bouddhisme du Bouddha, ses doctrines, ses méthodes et ses développements mahâyânistes et tantriques au Tibet. Paris, Plon, 1960.

Immortalité et réincarnation. Doctrines et pratiques. Chine-Tibet-Inde. Paris, Plon, 1961.

Quarante siècles d'expansion chinoise. Paris, Plon, 1964.

L'Inde où j'ai vécu. Avant et après l'Indépendance. Paris, Plon, 1969 (Augmented edition of *L'Inde. Hier-aujourd'hui-demain*).

Grammaire de la langue tibétaine parlée, posthumous, published by Marie-Madeleine Peyronnet.

En Chine. L'Amour universel et l'individualisme intégral. Les maîtres Mo-tse et Yang-tchou. Paris, Plon, 1970.

Le Sortilège du mystère. Faits étranges et gens bizarres rencontrés au long de mes routes d'Orient et d'Occident. Paris, Plon, 1972.

Journal de voyage. Lettres à son mari. Paris, Plon, 1976.

Vivre au Tibet : cuisine, traditions et images. Morel éditeur, 1975.

Voyages et aventures de l'esprit, textes et documents inédits. Paris, Plon, 1973.

Articles by Alexandra David-Néel under Other Names

"Réponse à la tribune théosophique," *Le Lotus bleu: revue théosophique mensuelle*, 4ᵉannée, n°8, 27 octobre 1893, pp.205-210

"Notes sur le bouddhisme," *L'Étoile socialiste*, 1895

"De l'importance des influences ambiantes au point de vue philosophique," *Alliance scientifique universelle*, 1900

"Un mot sur le bouddhisme," *Revue de sociologie et d'ethnographie*, 1901

"Les mantras aux Indes," *Bulletins et Mémoires de la Société Anthropologique de Paris*, 1901

"De l'origine physique des mythes et de leur influence sur les institutions sociales," *L'Idée libre*, 1901

"Les congrégations en Chine," *Mercure de France*, 1903

"Conférence de Madame Néel (Myrial)," *Régénération, Organe de la ligue de la régénération humaine*, 1903

"De l'entraînement psychique dans les sectes yoguistes," *Bulletins et Mémoires de la Société Anthropologique de Paris*, 1904

"Le pouvoir religieux au Thibet: ses origines," *Mercure de France*, 1904

"Le clergé thibétain et ses doctrines," *Mercure de France*, 1904

"Religions et superstitions coréennes," *Mercure de France*, 1904

"Notes historiques sur la Corée," *Mercure de France*, 1904

"Les moines soldats de l'armée coréenne," *L'Européen*, 1904

"La séparation : Chez les Protestants," *L'Européen*, 1905

"La question religieuse au Japon: la séparation des Églises et de l'État," *Mercure de France*, 1905

"Moukden, notes historiques," *Mercure de France*, 1905

"Allocution sur la morale laïque," *Congrès de la libre pensée*, 1905

"La séparation et les protestants français," *Le Courrier européen*, 1906

"Une Jeanne d'Arc annamite," *Mercure de France*, 1907

"Le pacifisme dans l'Antiquité chinoise," *Mercure de France*, 1907

"Notes sur la philosophie japonaise," *La Nouvelle Société*, 1907

"L'instruction des indigènes en Tunisie (opinion de la jeunesse intellectuelle musulmane), *Mercure de France*, 1908

"Les colonies Sionistes en Palestine," *Mercure de France*, 1909

"Buddhism and social problems," *The Buddhist Review*, 1910

"Auprès du Dalaï-Lama," *Mercure de France*, 1912

"Notes sur le Mahayana," *Le Lotus bleu*, 1913

"Les statues de Vajrabhairava : au temple des lamas à Pékin," *Le politique de Pékin*, 1918

"L'Inde avec les Anglais," *Mercure de France*, 1920

"La question du Thibet," *Mercure de France*, 1920

"L'Iliade thibétaine et ses bardes," *Mercure de France*, 1923

"Sur la route de Lhasa," *Le Lotus bleu*, 1924

"Le bouc émissaire des Thibétains," *Mercure de France*, 1924

"Les Thibétains : leur mentalité et leur mœurs," conférence pour l'*Institut général psychologique*, 1925

"Vie religieuse: prophéties thibétaines," *La vie des peuples*, 1925

"Vie religieuse: prophéties thibétaines," *La vie des peuples*, 1925

"Le Thibet mystique," *La revue de Paris*, 1927

"Comment les Tibétains envisagent la mort" (par Yongden), *Cahiers de l'Etoile*, 1929

"Réponse de Madame Néel sur l'inquiétude contemporaine," *Cahiers de l'Etoile*, 1930

"Femmes au Thibet," *La revue de Paris*, 1931

"Le Thibet et le Dalaï-Lama," *La revue de Paris*, 1934

"L'effondrement des Blancs en Chine," *La revue de Paris*, 1938

"Monastères tibétains," au service de l'Union française, revue des troupes coloniales, 1947

"Naissance de l'écriture dans les civilisations anciennes," *Les cahiers d'Hermès*, 1947

"*Lhag Thong*. La vue intense," *La revue théosophique*, 1947

"Gandhi: un Saint ou un Sage," *France-Asie*, 1948

"Visite aux étudiants et lettrés tibétains," *Connaissance du monde*, 1948

"Quelques mots sur le Shaktisme," *France-Asie*, 1949

"Le véritable visage du Tibet," *France-Asie*, 1950

"L'Inde au lendemain de l'Indépendance," *La revue des deux mondes*, 1951

"Le roman du bosquet du lotus," plusieurs épisodes, *France-Asie*, 1952

"Les marchands tibétains," *France-Asie*, 1953

"Les Abominables hommes des Neige," *France-Asie*, 1954

"*Samskaras*," *La Pensée bouddhique*, 1954

"Réflexions sur la discipline spirituelle bouddhique," *France-Asie*, 1957

"Anthropophagie rituelle contemporaine," *Connaissance du monde*, 1958

Books about Alexandra David-Néel

BROSSE, Jacques. *Alexandra David-Néel*. Paris, Albin Michel, 1978.

CHALON, Jean. *Le lumineux destin d'Alexandra David-Néel*. Paris, Perrin, 1998.

DÉSIRÉ-MARCHAND, Joëlle. *Les itinéraires d'Alexandra David-Néel: de Paris à Lhasa, de l'aventure à la sagesse*. Paris, Arthaud, 1998.

Alexandra David-Néel: vie et voyages. Itinéraires géographiques et spirituels. Paris, Arthaud, 2011.

FOSTER, Barbara, FOSTER, Michael. *Forbidden Journey: The Life of Alexandra David-Néel*. Harper Collins, 1987.

LESIEUR, Jennifer. *Alexandra David-Néel*. Paris, Gallimard, 2013.

MIDDLETON, Ruth. *Alexandra David-Néel: Portrait of an Adventurer*. Shambhala Publications, 2014.

PEYRONNET, Marie-Madeleine. *Dix ans avec Alexandra David Néel*. Paris, Plon, 1975.

VAN GRASDORFF, Gilles. *Alexandra David-Néel*. Paris, Pygmalion, 2011.

Secondary Sources

ALMOND, Philip. *The British Discovery of Buddhism*. Cambridge University Press, 1988.

APP, Urs. *The Birth of Orientalism*. University of Pennsylvania Press, 2010.

The Cult of Emptiness: The Western Discovery of Buddhist Thought and the Invention of Oriental Philosophy. University Media, 2012.

BECHERT, Heinz. *Buddhismus, Staat und Geselchaft in der Ländern des Theravada*

Buddhismus (1966)

BERLANSTEIN, Lenard R. *Daughters of Eve – A Cultural History of French Theater Women from the Old Regime to the Fin-de-siècle*. Harvard University Press, 2001.

BISHOP, Peter. *Dreams of Power: Tibetan Buddhism and the Western Imagination*. London, The Athlone Press, 1993.

The Myth of Shangri-la: Tibet, Travel-writing and the Western Creation of Sacred Landscape. Berkeley, University of California Press, 1989.

BRAUEN, Martin. *Dreamworld Tibet, Western Illusions*. Bangkok, Orchid Press Publishing, 2004.

BURNOUF, Eugène. *Introduction à l'histoire du bouddhisme indien*. Paris, Maisonneuve, 1844-1876; English translation: BUFFETRILLE, Katia, LOPEZ, Donald S., *Introduction to the history of the indian Buddhism*., Chicago, The University of Chicago Press, 2010.

DEBAENE, Vincent. *Far afield: French Anthropology Between Science and Literature*. Chicago University Press, 2014.

DELALANDE, Marie-José. "Le movement théosophique en France (1876-1921)," PhD Dissertation, Faculté de lettres, langues et sciences humaines, Université du Maine, 2007.

DODIN, Thierry, RATHER, Heinz (ed.). *Imagining Tibet: perceptions, projections and fantasies*. Chicago, Wisdom Publications Inc., 1993.

ESTELMANN, Frank, MOUSSA, Sarga, WOLFZETTEL, Friedrich (ed.). *Voyageuses européennes au XIXe siècle. Identités, genres, codes*. Paris, Presses universitaires Paris Sorbonne, 2012.

FRANKLIN, Jeffrey. *Lotus and the Lion: Buddhism and the British Empire*. Cornell University Press, 2008.

HACKETT, Paul G. *Theos Bernard, The White Lama: Tibet, Yoga, and American Religious Life*. Columbia University Press, 2012.

HAMMER, Olav. *Claiming Knowledge: Strategies of Epistemology from Theosophy to the New Age*. Numen Book Series 90, Brill Academic Publishings, 2003.

HANNAM, June. *Feminism*. London, Routedge, 2006.

HANEGRAAFF, Wouter. *New Age Religion and Western Culture: Esotericism in the Mirror of Secular Thought*. Leiden/New York, State University of New York Press, 1996.

Esotericism and the Academy: Rejected Knowledge in Western Culture. Cambridge University Press, 2012.

Western Esotericism : A Guide for the Perplexed. London, Bloomsbury, 2013.

HARVEY, David Allen. *Beyond Enlightenment: Occultism and Politics in Modern France*. Northern Illinois University Press, 2005.

HODGSON, Barbara. *Dreaming of East: Western women and the exotic allure of the Orient*. Douglas and McIntyre, 2005.

KING, Richard, *Orientalism and Religion: Post-Colonial Theory, India and "The Mystic East."* London, Routledge, 1999.

LACHAPELLE, Sophie. *Investigating the Supernatural: From Spiritism and Occultism to Psychical Research and Metapsychics in France, 1853-1931*. Johns Hopkins University Press, 2011.

LAURANT, Jean-Pierre. *René Guénon: les enjeux d'une lecture*. Paris, Dervy, 2006.

Le Regard ésotérique. Paris, Bayard, 2001.

LAVOIE, Jeffrey D. *The Theosophical Society: History of a Spiritualist Movement*. Boca Raton, Brown Walker Press, 2012.

LE CALLOC'H, Bernard, "Un couple d'explorateurs en Asie centrale: Charles et Marie de Ujfalvy de Mezökövesd," *Mondes et cultures. Comptes rendus trimestriels des séances de l'Académie des sciences d'Outre-mer*, n°46/2, 1986, pp.299-313.

LOPEZ, Donald S. *Prisoners of Shangrila: Tibetan Buddhism and the West*. University of Chicago Press, 1999.

Curators of the Buddha, The Study of Buddhism under Colonialism, Chicago, The University of Chicago Press, 1995.

Buddhism and Science, A Guide for the Perplexed. University of Chicago Press, 2010.

A Modern Buddhist Bible. Boston, Beacon Press, 2002.

From Stone to Flesh: A Short History of the Buddha. University of Chicago Press, 2013.

MARTIN, Xavier. *Nature humaine et révolution française: Du Siècle des Lumières au Code Napoléon*, 3e édition, Poitiers, Dominique Martin Morin, 2015 (1st ed. 1994).

Translated as *Human Nature and the French Revolution: From the Enlightenment to the Napoleonic Code*, trans. P. Corcoran. Berghahn Books, New York-Oxford, 2001.

Naissance du sous-homme au cœur des Lumières : Les races, les femmes, le peuple. Poitiers, Dominique Martin Morin, 2014.

MATHER SAUL, Jennifer. *Feminism: Issues and Arguments*, Oxford, Oxford University Press, 2003.

MASUZAWA, Tomoko, *The Invention of World Religions: Or how European universalism was preserved in the language of pluralism*. University of Chicago Press, 2005.

MCMAHAN, David. *The Making of Buddhist Modernism*. Oxford University Press, 2008.

MESCH, Rachel. *Having It All in the Belle Epoque: How French Women's Magazines Invented the Modern Woman*. Stanford University Press, 2013.

The Hysterics' Revenge: French Women Writers at the Fin de Siècle. Vanderbilt University Press, 2006.

MONROE, John Warne. *Laboratories of Faith: Mesmerism, Spiritism, and Occultism in Modern France.* Cornell University Press, 2007.

OPPENHEIM, Janet. *The Other World: Spiritualism and Psychical Research in England 1850-1914.* Cambridge University Press, 1985.

OWEN, Alex. *The Darkened Room: Women, Power, and Spiritualism in Late Victorian England*, Chicago. University of Chicago Press, 2004.

The Place of Enchantment: British Occultism and the Culture of the Modern. University of Chicago Press, 2007.

PREBISH Charles, BAUMANN Martin (ed.). *Westward Dharma: Buddhism Beyond Asia.* Berkeley, University of California Press, 2002.

PROTHERO, Stephen R. *The White Buddhist: The Asian Odyssey of Henry Steel Olcott.* Bloomington, Indiana University Press, 1996.

RÉMOND, René. *Histoire de l'anticléricalisme en France de 1815 à nos jours.* Paris, Fayard, 1976.

Religion et société en Europe: La secularization au XIXe et XXe siècles (1789-2000). Paris, Seuil, 1996.

STRUBBE, Julian. "Occultist Identity Formations Between Theosophy and Socialism in *fin-de-siècle* France." *Numen*, September 2016.

SHARP, Lynn L. *Secular Spirituality: Reincarnation and Spiritism in nineteenth-century France.* Lexington Books, 2006.

THEVOZ Samuel. *Un horizon infini: Explorateurs et voyageurs français au Tibet 1846-1912.* Paris, Presses Universitaires Paris Sorbonne, 2010.

THEVOZ Samuel. "Une 'étrange nature': l'exploration du Baltistan ou l'émergence d'un imaginaire feminine dans *Le voyage d'une Parisienne dans l'Himalaya* de Marie de Ujfalvy-Bourdon." *Travaux de literature, Itinéraires littéraires du voyage*, XXVI, 2013.

UJFALVY-BOURDON, Marie de. *De Paris à Samarkand : impressions de voyage d'une Parisienne.* Paris, Hachette, 1880.

Voyage d'une Parisienne dans l'Himalaya. Paris, Transboréal, 2014.

REFERENCES

1 Alexandra David-Néel, *Le modernisme bouddhiste et le bouddhisme du Bouddha*, Paris, Alcan, 1911.

2 Jacques Brosse, *Alexandra David-Néel, L'aventure et la spiritualité*, Paris, Retz, 1978, re-ed. Albin Michel, 1991, Jean Chalon, *Le lumineux destin d'Alexandra David-Néel*, Paris, Perrin, 1985; Ruth Middleton, *Alexandra David-Néel, Portrait of an Adventurer*, Boston, Shambhala, 1989 ; Barbara Foster and Michael Foster, *The secret lives of Alexandra David-Néel : a biography of the explorer of Tibet and its forbidden practices*, Boston, Shambhala, 1998; Joëlle Désiré-Marchand, *Les itinéraires d'Alexandra David-Néel*, Paris, Arthaud, 1996, re-ed. 2009; Joëlle Désiré-Marchand,*Tibet, voyage à Lhassa, sur les traces d'Alexandra David-Néel* (photographies de Stefano Ponsotti), Arthaud, 2004; Joëlle Désiré-Marchand, *Alexandra David-Néel, Vie et voyages*, Paris, Arthaud, 2009 ; Joëlle Désiré-Marchand, *Alexandra David-Néel, passeur pour notre temps*, Paris, Le Passeur, 2016 ; Gilles van Grasdorff, *Alexandra David-Néel*, Paris, Pygmalion, 2011; Jennifer Lesieur, *Alexandra David-Néel* , Paris, Folio Gallimard, 2013; Laure Dominique Agniel, *Alexandra David-Néel , exploratrice et féministe*, Paris, Tallandier, 2018; Jeanne Mascolo de Filippis et Antoine de Maximy, *Alexandra David-Néel* , Paris, Paulsen, 2018. To those books one should add several scholarly articles and many documentary and fictional movies, theater plays, cartoons, and animated tales.

3 David McMahan, *The Making of Buddhist Modernism*, Oxford, Oxford University Press, 2008. The term 'Buddhist Modernism' as a concept characterizing recent transformations of Buddhism is actually borrowed from Heinz Bechert, *Buddhismus, Staat und Geselchaft in der Ländern des Theravada Buddhismus*, vol. 1, Berlin, Alfred Metzner, 1966 and Heinz Bechert, Richard Gombrich (ed.), "Buddhist Revival in East and West," in *The World of Buddhism*, London, Thames and Hudson, 1991, pp.273-285.

4 Donald S. Lopez, *A Modern Buddhist Bible*, Boston, Beacon Press, 2002, Introduction, pp. xxxix and x. Alexandra David-Néel is cited among the modern Buddhists of the book, and an excerpt of her *Magic and Mystery in Tibet* (1971) is offered (pp.59-67)

5 Heinz Bechert, Buddhismus, Staat, und Gesellschaft in der Ländern des Theravada-Buddhismus, 3 vols., O. Harrassowitz, Wiesbaden, 1966-1973.

6 Charles Taylor, *The Sources of the Self: The Making of the Modern Identity*, Harvard University Press, 1989.

7 Wiktor Stoczkowski in *Anthropologies rédemptrices. Le monde selon Lévi-Strauss*, Paris, Hermann, 2008, p.79 ff. The author explains that the term soteriological (from the Greek *sôtêria*, which refers to the idea of preservation, conservation, or setting apart from evil) can be heuristically used to describe all sorts of discourses, even apparently scientific or neutral, that actually consists in a theory of evil, instead of explaining a reality – or, in the case of modern Buddhists, discourses that develop a whole theory on the calamitous state of man in modern societies instead of defining and exposing Buddhist doctrines such as karma, co-dependent origination, samsara, Buddha nature, enlightenment, Four Noble Truths, or the Noble Eightfold Path, etc.

8 Stephen Prothero, *The White Buddhist. The Asian Odyssey of Henry Steel Olcott*, Indiana University Press, 1996.

9 P. Chevallier, *La Séparation de l'Église et de l'École*, Paris, Fayard, 1981; J.M. Mayeur, *La Vie politique sous la IIIe République*, Paris, Seuil, 1984, *La Séparation de l'Église et de l'État*, Paris, Julliard, 1966.

10 Georges Dupeux, "La IIIe République, 1871-1914," pp. 738-763, in Georges Duby (ed.), *Histoire de la France des origines à nos jours*, Paris, Larousse, 1999.

11 On Anticlericalism and French Free Thought in the 19th and 20th centuries: René Rémond, *Religion et société en Europe aux XIXe et XXe siècles. Essai sur la sécularisation*, Paris, Seuil, 1996; René Rémond, *L'Anticléricalisme en France de 1815 à nos jours*, Paris, Fayard, 1976; Jacqueline Lalouette, *La libre pensée en France, 1848-1940*, Paris, Albin Michel, 1997.

12 Archives départementales d'Indre et Loire, "Louis Pierre David (1815-1904), Un Tourangeau opposant républicain au coup d'État de Napoléon III, père de l'aventurière et exploratrice Alexandra David-Néel (1868-1969)," available online: http://archives.cg37.fr/Outil/LOUIS_PIERRE_DAVID,_PERE_DE_L_AVENTURIERE_ALEXANDRA_DAVID_NEEL_-ADEW.html.

13 Alexandra David-Néel , *Correspondance avec son mari*, March, 19, 1913.

14 Alexandra David-Néel , unpublished letters to her husband, December 1904, Archives of the David-Néel 's Museum in Digne-les-Bains. She notably mentioned how she quarrelled with her mother about the kind of funeral they should arrange for her father. The mother insisted that they follow the Catholic rites, whereas she, sharing her father's beliefs, wanted a freemason ceremony.

15 See the work of Xavier Martin, notably *Naissance du sous-homme au cœur des Lumières. Les races, les femmes, le peuple*, Poitiers, Dominique Martin Morin, 2014.

16 Julian Strube, "Socialist religion and the emergence of occultism: a genealogical approach to socialism and secularization in 19th century France," *Religion*, 2016, and "Occultist Identity Formations Between Theosophy and Socialism in fin-de-siècle France," *Numen*, 2016.

17 James Webb, The Flight from Reason, London, Macdonald and Co., 1971, Christopher McIntosh, Éliphas Lévi and the French Occult Revival, 2d ed., London, Rider, 1975, Wouter Hanegraaff, Esotericism and the Academy : Rejected Knowledge in

Western Culture, Cambridge, Cambridge University Press, 2012.

18   Arnaud de l'Étoile, Éliphas Lévi, Qui suis-je?, Grèz-sur-Loing, Éditions Pardès, 2008, p.27.

19   Pierre Chevallier, *Histoire de la Franc-Maçonnerie française, tome 3: La Maçonnerie, Église de la République (1877-1944)*, Paris, Fayard, 1993.

20   Augustin Chaboseau is also the author of a book on Buddhism: *Essai sur la philosophie bouddhique*, Paris, Flammarion, 1891.

21   Julian Strube, op.cit., p.8.

22   'Gnostic' here should be understood in the sense given to the term by April DeConick in *The Gnostic New Age: How a Countercultural Spirituality Revolutionized Religion from Antiquity to Today*, New York, Columbia University Press, 2016: a spiritual approach of the divine based on the belief that God is to be found within each individual, and reached through ecstatic union rather than delivered by an institution.

23   Papus, *Anarchie, Indolence et Synarchie. Les lois physiologiques d'organisation sociale et l'ésotérisme* ("Anarchy, Indolence, and Synarchy. The Physiological Laws of Social Organisation and Esotericism"), Paris, Chamuel, 1894.

24   Alexandra David-Néel, *Le sortilège du mystère*, op.cit., pp.11-12. See translated excerpts in Appendix.

25   Alexandra David-Néel, *Lampe de sagesse*, op.cit., p.14.

26   Ibid., p.13.

27   Ibid., p.16.

28   Paris, Librairie Perrin, 1889. English edition: Édouard Schuré, *The Great Initiates: A Study of the Secret History of Religions*, Harper Collins, 1980 (re-ed ?). The book has constantly been reissued and seems to be widely read. It has been published as a modern French paperback edition as The Bible of Esotericism (Edition Pocket).

29   The theme of despair was treated by many European intellectuals at the turn of the century, from different perspectives: philosophical, literary, artistic, and scientific (psychological and sociological). In France, the founder of Sociology, Émile Durkheim, published his famous book on suicide in 1897. Contrary to Schuré and other spiritualists, he attributed desperation not to a lack of existential meaning, but to the loosening of social control over individuals by religious institutions.

30   Marie-José Delalande, op.cit.

31   Pierre Mollier, Sylvie Bourel, Laurent Portes (ed.), *La franc-maçonnerie*, Paris, Bibliothèque Nationale de France – BNF, 2016 ; Roger Dachez et Alain Bauer, *La franc-maçonnerie*, Paris, Presses Universitaires de France, coll. Que sais-je? 2016 (re-ed.) ; Jean-Claude Lozac'hmeur, *Les origines occultistes de la Franc-maçonnerie*, Paris, Éditions des Cimes, 2015 and *Fils de la Veuve: Recherches sur l'ésotérisme maçonnique*, Paris, Éditions de Chiré, 2002; Roger Dachez, *Histoire de la franc-maçonnerie française*, Paris, Presses Universitaires de France, coll. Que sais-je?, 2003;

Christian Doumergue et Alain Bauer, *Franc-maçonnerie et histoire de France*, Paris, Éditions de l'Opportun, 2016; Pierre Mollier, *La Chevalerie maçonnique: Franc-maçonnerie, imaginaire chevaleresque et légende templière au siècle des Lumières*, Paris, Dervy, 2005 ; Collectif, *Encyclopédie de la franc-maçonnerie*, Paris, Le Livre de Poche, 2002; André Combe, *Histoire de la Franc-maçonnerie au XIXe siècle*, t.1 et t.2, Paris, Éditions du Rocher, 1998-1999; Paul Gourdot, *Les sources maçonniques du socialisme français (1848-1871)*, Paris, Éditions du Rocher, 1998.

32 A rite of passage, a synonym for initiation, consists in the celebration of the passage, for an individual or a small group, from one society or one group within the society to another. At the end of the process, which includes purification and hardship, the individual gains a new identity. Ethnologists have written extensively on the subject. A seminal definition can be found in Arnold Van Gennep, *Les rites de passage*, Paris, Emile Nourry, 1909.

33 The link between the Freemasons and the establishment of the Republic in France is well-known, the political nature of the Theosophical Society, however, is less frequently noted. See Mark Bevir, "Theosophy as a Political Movement," in A. Copley (ed.), *Gurus and the Followers: New Religious Reform Movements in Colonial India*, Delhi, Oxford University Press, 2000. It is also worth noting that all the initiates mentioned by Schuré in his book are social reformer as much as religious thinkers.

34 The obsession with human regeneration, which is perhaps the main characteristic of 'modernity', is a product of the Enlightenment philosophers, who reinterpreted human history and Christian theology in medical terms. See Xavier Martin, *Régénérer l'espèce humaine: utopie médicale et Lumières*, Poitiers, Dominique Martin Morin, 2008.

35 This 'esoteric' approach to religious diversity purported by spiritualists in the 19th century can be seen as an immanent (or atheistic) replacement of the previous Christian ways to look at religious otherness. In previous centuries, other religions had mainly been understood by Europeans as either demonic or as various cases of 'natural religion', that is to say cultures that promoted good morality and a sense of the divine, although they were not taught the Gospels, for obvious historical or geographical reasons. The European attitude towards religions started to change and become more systematic and less polemical in the early 18th century, notably through the work of two French Protestant refugees, Jean-Frédéric Bernard and Bernard Picart, in their *Religious Ceremonies of the World* (1733-1737). This collection of books was immensely successful and was probably the first encyclopaedic approach to religions. See Lynn Hunt, Margaret C. Jacob, and Wijnand Mijnhardt, *The Book That Changed Europe: Picart and Bernard's Religious Ceremonies of the World*, Belknap Press, 2010. In a way, the 19th-century 'esoteric' understanding of religious diversity is an attempt to reunify, within a single spiritual worldview, the pluralistic descriptions of religious rituals by early Enlightenment thinkers. It is typical of the 19th century's turn of mind in that it tried to identify a common origin to the diverse religions one could observe throughout the historical and geographical spectrum – just as Darwin tried to identify a common ancestor to the variety of living and dead animal species.

36 As established about Alexandra David-Néel and Victor Segalen by Samuel Thevoz in *'Au bord d'un mystère': de Ceylan au Tibet, Alexandra David-Néel ,Victor Segalen et le bouddhisme.*

37 Alexandra David-Néel, *Le sortilège du mystère,* op.cit., p.9.

38 Ibid., pp.11-12

39 Ibid., p.10

40 Ibid., p.10

41 Ibid., pp.17-19 (translated excerpt in Appendix).

42 Ibid.

43 Ibid., p.26 and pp.38-39.

44 Ibid., pp.35-37.

45 Ibid., p.41.

46 A Theosophical branch is a group composed of at least 7 members. A section is composed of 7 branches.

47 Alfred Percy Sinnett published *Esoteric Buddhism* in 1883. The book is a synthesis of the Theosophical view of the cosmos, the spiritual (rather than purely biological) evolution of man, the role of the 'esoteric teachers' in humans' way to perfection, a specific definition of 'science' (which opposes democracy and discussion), and a Theosophical interpretation of teachings attributed to the Buddha.

48 Stephen Prothero, *The White Buddhist: The Asian Odyssey of Henry Steel Olcott*, Bloomington, Indiana University Press, 1996.

49 Marie-Josée Delalande, "Le mouvement théosophique en France (1876-1921)." PhD thesis in History, Faculté de lettres, langues et sciences humaines, Université du Maine, 2007.

50 See Muriel Pécastaing-Boissière, *Annie Besant (1847-1933): la lutte et la quête,* Paris, Adyar, 2015.

51 *Le sortilège du mystère,* op.cit., p.42.

52 Ibid., pp.42-46.

53 Some descriptions by 19th-century European occultists of their previous lives on various planets can be found in Alex Owen, *The Place of Enchantment: British Occultism and the Culture of the Modern*, Chicago, Chicago University Press, 2004, and in French in *Des Indes à la planète Mars: Étude sur un cas de somnambulisme avec glossolalie,* Paris, Alcan, 1900, by the famous Swiss medical doctor and psychologist Théodore Flournoy.

54 Ibid., pp.47-48. On the belief in extra-terrestrials as spiritual masters of mankind, see Wiktor Stoczkowski, *Des hommes, des dieux et des extraterrestres*, Paris, Flammarion, 1999.

55 *Le sortilège du mystère,* op.cit., pp.48-50.

56   Helena Petrovna Blavatsky, *Secret Instructions To Probators Of An Esoteric Occult School* (re-ed. 1969) and *The Voice of Silence*, 1889.

57   *Le sortilège du mystère*, op.cit., pp.51-53.

58   Mitra, "Réponse à l'article de Léon de Rosny," *Le Lotus bleu : revue théosophique mensuelle*, 4ᵉ année, n°8, 27 octobre 1893 (An 4995 du Kali-Yug), pp.205-210 ; Mitra, "Notes sur le bouddhisme," *L'Étoile socialiste*, 2ᵉ année, n°20, 18-25 avril 1895, p.1 ; Mitra, "Un mot sur le bouddhisme," *Revue de sociologie et d'ethnographie*, Paris, 1901, pp.3-5.

59   The two unpublished feminist novels are Alexandra David's *Le Grand Art* and *Dans la vie*. For the list of other periodical publications, see bibliography. Several conference papers she gave at the Theosophical Society (mostly in London) are kept in the archives at her museum in Digne.

60   Alexandra David-Néel , "Lettre à M. Devaux, professeur à la faculté de Bordeaux," 1909, published in *Lampe de sagesse*, Paris, Editions du Rocher, 2006 (1st ed. 1986), pp.83-85.

61   Alexandra David-Néel , *Correspondance avec son mari*, Letter from Rajahmundry, December 30, 1911, op.cit., pp.103-108.

62   Alexandra David, "Auprès du Dalaï Lama," Paris, *Mercure de France*, n°367, tome XCIX, October 1st, 1912, pp.466-476.

63   Alexandra David, "Au Pays du Bouddha," unpublished text. Archives of Alexandra David-Néel 's museum.

64   Friedrich Max Müller, *Nineteen Century*, London, 1893, pp.767-788. See Donald Lopez, *Buddhism and Science. A Guide for the Perplexed*, Chicago, The University of Chicago Press, 2008, pp.178-180.

65   Léon de Rosny, "Les théosophes et les mahatamas," *La Fraternité*, 3ᵉ année, n°33, Paris, 1ᵉʳ août 1893, p.4.

66   Léon de Rosny, *La méthode conscientielle, essai de philosophie exactiviste*, Paris, F. Alcan, 1887. On de Rosny: Bénédicte Fabre-Muller, Pierre Leboulleux, Philippe Rothstein, *Léon de Rosny (1837-1914), De l'Orient à l'Amérique*, Lille, Presses universitaires du Septentrion, 2014.

67   Léon de Rosny, *Le bouddhisme éclectique*, Paris, Ernest Leroux, 1894.

68   The idea that habits and characters depend on the environment in which people live already existed among the ancient Greeks and was common in Europe from the 16th century. It became very popular in the 18th century with the work of Montesquieu, who applied this theory to the realm of politics. Later, geographical determinism became a central tenet of anthropology, since it gave a solution to the biggest problem anthropologists had to face – the conciliation of cultural diversity with the belief in the unity of the human species.

69   Mitra, "Réponse à la tribune théosophique," op.cit., p.205.

70   His name is mentioned in the short list of disciples given by de Rosny in his book *Eclectic Buddhism*, op.cit., p.119 : Frédéric Lawton, D. Maceron, Jacques Tasset, D. Eloffe.

71   Archives of the museum, picture n°DN 23.

72   Jules Bois, *Les petites religions de Paris*, Paris, 1894 (first published as a series of articles in *Le Figaro*).

73   Jules Bois, op.cit., "Le bouddhisme éclectique."

74   Léon de Rosny, *Le bouddhisme éclectique*, Introduction, p.viii.

75   Ibid., p.vi.

76   Henry Steel Olcott, *Buddhist Catechism*, 1881.

77   Léon de Rosny, op.cit., Introduction, p.ix.

78   Ibid., Introduction, pp.ix-xxiii.

79   Ibid., Introduction, p.xxxii.

80   Ibid., Introduction, p.xxxiii.

81   Ibid., p.1.

82   Ibid., p.5.

83   Hervé Beaumont, *Les aventures d'Émile Guimet, un industriel voyageur*, Paris, Arthaud, 2014.

84   Deliberation of the municipal council of the City Hall of Paris, March 16, 1885, quoted in Hervé Beaumont, op.cit., p.276-277.

85   Around 150 articles were published in the French and international press on the first two ceremonies (less on the third because of the Dreyfus Affair, which was overshadowing other topics). The École Française d'Extrême Orient's deputy librarian Antony Boussemart wrote an interesting article about these ceremonies and their reception by the public: "Un temple bouddhiste au cœur de Paris" in Françoise Chappuis and Francis Macouin, *D'Outremer et d'Orient mystique : les itinéraires d'Émile Guimet*, Paris, Findalky, 2001, pp.91-106, on which I rely here.

86   réf

87   Judith Snodgrass, *Presenting Japanese Buddhism to the West: Orientalism, Occidentalism, and the Columbian Exposition*, The University of North Carolina Press, 2003.

88   John Snelling, *Buddhism in Russia: The Story of Avgan Dorzhiev: Lhasa's Emissary to the Tsar*, Element Books, 1993.

89   Quoted in Antony Boussemart, op.cit., p.106.

90   Alexandra David-Néel , *L'Inde où j'ai vécu*, Paris, Plon, 1969, pp.9-10 (First published as *L'Inde. Hier, aujourd'hui, demain*, Paris, Plon, 1951).

91   Published in Jean Flechet, *Les voyages d'Alexandra David-Néel : Paroles d'une*

centenaire, Editions de Haute Provence, 1993, p.44.

92 In *L'Inde où j'ai vécu*, op.cit., pp.13-14, she says that her first trip to India in 1894 "was a religious act in the purest sense of the word," and that this act included "the continuation of the study of Sanskrit." The only period when she could have learned Sanskrit where courses were available (at the Sorbonne and the Collège de France) was 1893, after she had started living in Paris in December 1892 (at the Theosophical Society).

93 Mitra, "Notes sur le bouddhisme," op.cit., p.1.

94 Ibid.

95 Ibid.

96 Ibid.,

97 Alexandra Myrial, "Un mot sur le bouddhisme," op.cit., pp.3-5.

98 Ibid., p.3.

99 Alexandra Myrial, "De l'importance des influences ambiantes d'un point de vue philosophique," Paris, *Alliance scientifique universelle*, 1901, "De l'origine physique des mythes et de leur influence sur les institutions sociales," Paris-Bruxelles, *L'Idée libre*, 1901.

100 Alexandra David, "Notes sur le bouddhisme au Tonkin," Archives of the Alexandra David-Néel Museum.

101 Alexandra David, "Quelques écrivains bouddhistes contemporains," Paris, *Mercure de France*, 1909, pp.637-647.

102 Donald S. Lopez, *A Modern Buddhist Bible*, Boston, Beacon Press, 2002, Introduction, David McMahan, *The Making of Buddhist Modernism*, Oxford, Oxford University Press, 2008.

103 Alexandra David, "Quelques écrivains bouddhistes contemporains," op.cit., p.639.

104 Ibid., p.640.

105 Unpublished correspondence with her husband, Alexandra David-Néel's Museum in Digne-les-Bains.

106 Alexandra David, "Quelques écrivains bouddhistes contemporains," op.cit., p.643

107 Ibid., p.645.

108 Alexandra David-Néel, *Le modernisme bouddhiste ou le bouddhisme du Bouddha*, Paris, Alcan, 1911. The book was revised, with all the original political ideas removed, as *Le bouddhisme du Bouddha*, 1977. The 1911 version is no longer in print.

109 Ibid., p.17.

110 Ibid., p.18.

111 Ibid., p.210.

112 Ibid., p.117.

113 Ibid., pp.120-121.

114 Ibid., pp.122-123.

115 Ibid., p.124-128.

116 Ibid., pp.137-139.

117 Ibid., p.140.

118 Ibid., pp.163-188.

119 Ibid., pp.163-164.

120 Hendrik Kern, *Histoire du bouddhisme dans l'Inde*, translated into French by Gédéon Huet, Paris, Eernest Leroux, 1901, cited in Alexandra David, op.cit., p.190.

121 Ibid., p.191.

122 Ibid., pp.204-215.

123 Ibid., pp.210-215.

124 Other European thinkers with the same kind of occultist background also created hybrid forms of Buddhism based on recent descriptions of the world that constituted alternatives to Biblical stories. Alfred Percy Sinnett (1840-1921), for instance, composed his "esoteric Buddhism" (1883) with the Darwinian theory of evolution, Theosophical notions of "science," a spiritualist philosophy, and a few words of Buddhist vocabulary. The ideological matrix is the same – the wish to rewrite or completely replace the Christian conception and organization of the world. Alexandra David's specificity within the modernist Buddhist movement is perhaps to have privileged a political and rationalist dimension of this project, over that of science, which seems to have characterized English-speaking authors. This may be explained by her rejection of the Theosophical conceptions of both "science" and "esotericism," and by the French political tradition of "revolution."

125 Rémi Brague, *Modérément moderne*, Paris, Flammarion, 2014.

126 Alexandra David-Néel, *Correspondance avec son mari*, Paris, Plon, 1970, letter dated April 18, 1918, p.507 (my translation).

127 To take but a recent example, Jennifer Lesieur, *Alexandra David-Néel* op.cit., 2013, p.15 (my translation): "The basis of a fanatic laicism settles, which will not prevent her from admiring the Christ and from believing in something superior, immaterial, and inaccessible to the human spirit."

128 Alexandra Myrial, *Pour la Vie:* Réflexion sur tous les faits de société, Brussels, La Bibliothèque des Temps Nouveaux, 1900 (For Life: Reflection on Every Social Fact). The following notes refer to this book. See the Appendix to read my translations of all those quotes. Louise David used many pen names to publish her articles, pamphlets and books. 'Alexandra' seemed to have become her preferred first name, to which she added other invented or real family names: 'Myrial', based on a character from *Les Misérables* by Victor Hugo, the bishop Myriel, who, trying to convert a Socialist to Christianity, is himself converted to Socialism, David, and later David-Néel, a

combination of both her name and that of her husband. She also used mythical names from Eastern religious literature, such as Mitra.

129 Ibid., p.35.
130 Ibid., p.13
131 Ibid., p.66.
132 See note 11.
133 Ibid., p.72 and pp.66-67.
134 Ibid., p.69.
135 Ibid., pp.70-71.
136 Ibid., pp.74-75, Italics in the original text.
137 Ibid., pp.15-16.
138 Ibid., p.16.
139 Ibid., p.19.
140 Ibid., p.20.
141 Ibid., pp.38-39, p.64.
142 Ibid., p.64.
143 Ibid., p.43.
144 Ibid., p.44.
145 Ibid., p.49.
146 Ibid., p.49.
147 Ibid., p.49.
148 Ibid., p.19.
149 Ibid., p.30.
150 Ibid., p.37.
151 Ibid., p.63.
152 Ibid., p.71.
153 "Faillite," *La Fronde*, August 15, 1902, in *Alexandra David-Néel, Féministe et libertaire*, op.cit., p.120.
154 According to Marie-Madeleine Peyronnet, who found the text in a cabinet, Alexandra David-Néel wanted to re-publish the text a few years before her death, claiming it was her intellectual testament. David-Néel herself confirms in her writings that she did not change her mind about what she wrote in *Pour la Vie* in 1898: "I remember that I wrote, in the surroundings of Hyères, at the Mediterranean seaside, a pamphlet that had some success since it was translated into three or four languages. It was entitled 'Pour la Vie.' I repudiate nothing of what I said therein," in Alexandra

David-Néel , *Correspondance avec son mari (1904-1941)*, Paris, Plon, 2000 (2nd edition), p.477, and "One will *live, be*. I wrote 'Pour la Vie' a long time ago and I do not withdraw. The one who believes in 'me' cannot but have this fierce motto: 'Let the Universe perish, if that entails saving 'me,' my life!' And this motto, consciously or unconsciously, is inscribed in the heart of everyone," Ibid., p.563.

155 Xavier Martin, *Nature humaine et Révolution française: Du Siècle des Lumières au Code Napoléon*, 3ᵉ édition, Poitiers, Dominique Martin Morin, 2015 (1st ed. 1994), translated as *Human Nature and the French Revolution: From the Enlightenment to the Napoleonic Code*, trans. P. Corcoran, Berghahn Books, New York-Oxford, 2001.

156 On the endless discussions the Encyclopaedists had on the questions of humanity (according to them an intellectual concept deprived of any tangible reality) and the thinking beings (a scarce minority to which they belonged): Xavier Martin, *Naissance du sous-homme au cœur des Lumières.* Op.cit.

157 Posthumously published as Alexandra David-Néel, *La lampe de sagesse,* Paris, éditions du Rocher, 1986.

158 In *Le Sortilège du mystère*, Paris, Plon, 1972 (posthumous), she describes the secret societies she belonged to when she was in her twenties, including the Theosophical Society. The tone of her writing and the explanations she gives to her being there are obviously a re-interpretation of an unassumed past. There is so much irony in her descriptions that the reader is left to wonder why she ever got there in the first place.

159 Alexandra David-Néel, *Le sortilège du mystère*, Paris, Plon, 1972.

160 Ibid., p.18.

161 The mid-19th century was marked, in European Catholic countries, by a renewal of the traditional faith, explained by the Catholics' reaction to the rationalists' attacks, the political situation in Italy, the creation of new congregations, the multiplication of Marial apparitions (Paris, 1830, Rome, 1842, La Salette, 1846, Lourdes, 1858), and the modern organization of international pilgrimages that followed. According to the historian Ruth Harris in *Lourdes: Body and Spirit in the Secular Age*, London, Penguin, 1999, this Catholic revival should not be understood as the accidental and anachronistic resurgence of ancient superstitions, but as another expression of the modern quest for the 'self,' with all its scientific, medical and theatrical dimensions.

162 The Sulpician Style was an expression invented in 1897 by the polemicist and writer Léon Bloy to designate the simple and insipid style so typical of the statues and stained glass of the Saint Sulpice Church in the 6th arrondissement of Paris – which we would call "kitsch" today, with its cheap materials, watery colors, and sentimental expressions. It became a derogatory term to describe the religious sensitivity of the late 19th century, characterized by its extreme sentimentalism, mostly associated with women. It is one of the reasons why many men and a few progressive women like Louise David could not subscribe to Catholicism anymore. See Ralph Gibson, "Le catholicisme et les femmes en France au XIXe siècle," *Revue d'histoire de l'Église de*

France, tome 79, n°202, 1993, pp.63-93.

163 With all the spiritualist and messianic dimensions of earlier socialism being transferred into so-called "occult societies" and labelled by the new, dominant Marxist trends as "utopian" – which explains why so many Socialists joined esoteric movements, Cf Julian Strube, "Socialism and Esotericism in July Monarchy France" in *History of Religion*, July 2016 and "Occultist Identity Formations Between Theosophy and Socialism in Fin-de-Siècle France," *Numen*, September 2016.

164 Jacqueline Lalouette, "De quelques aspects de l'athéisme en France au XIXe siècle," *Cahiers d'histoire*, n°87 : Religion et culture au XIXe siècle en France, 2002, pp.81-100; Dominique Morin, *L'athéisme moderne*, Paris, Cerf, 1985.

165 Ernest Renan famously published *The Life of Jesus (La vie de Jésus)* in 1863, in which he explained that Jesus was a historic person, a man and not a God, rejected the veracity of the Gospels regarding miracles and claimed that Jesus 'aryanized' Judaism, that is to say purified that religion from its "absurdities" and "Semitic heaviness."

166 Jean Richepin, *Les Blasphèmes*, 1884. His contemporary and friend, the writer Léon Bloy, said that Richepin "did not care about anything, except two things: having as much pleasure as possible and making noise in the world" (Léon Bloy, *Lettre à Jean Richepin*, 1877).

167 Jacqueline Lalouette, op.cit.

168 Jean Richepin, *Les blasphèmes*, Paris, 1884, Foreword, http://gallica.bnf.fr/ark:/12148/bpt6k549860.r=Richepin.langFR.

169 Elisée Reclus' major geographic works are *The Earth and Its Inhabitants (La Terre et ses habitants)*, six volumes, 1876-1894.

170 "Blue notebook," archives of the David-Néel museum.

171 "Pourquoi sommes-nous anarchistes?" *La Société nouvelle*, année 5, Tome 2, Paris-Bruxelles, 1889, http://gallica.bnf.fr/ark:/12148/bpt6k1025182g.

172 Archive of the University found and published by Gilles van Grasdorff, op.cit. The year, however, is not mentioned.

173 Max Stirner, *The Ego and Its Own*, 1845.

174 On the philosophers' and revolutionaries' conception of women, see Xavier Martin, *Naissance du sous-homme,* op.cit., and Louis Devance, "Le féminisme pendant la Révolution française," *Annales historiques de la révolution française*, n°229, 1997, pp.341-376.

175 Although faith and tradition were eroded by the industrial revolution, and many workers left the Church, most women in the 19th century were still profoundly Catholic, both among peasants and the middle and upper-classes. The majority of French feminists were actually conservative Catholics, and wished to promote a vision of womanhood in tune with the Christian teachings. See Bruno Dumons, *Les Dames de la Ligue des Femmes Françaises (1901-1914)*, Paris, Cerf, 2006.

176 This idea of the Church's responsibility in the 'oppression of women' has been refuted by more recent historiography. See See Ralph Gibson, "Le catholicisme et les femmes au XIXe siècle," *Revue d'histoire de l'Église de France*, tome 79, n°202, 1993, pp.63-93, and Régine Pernoud, *La Femme au temps des cathédrales*, Paris, Stock, 1980.

177 Jean-Louis Debré et Valérie Bochenek, *Ces femmes qui ont réveillé la France*, Paris, Arthème Fayard, 2013, *Maria Deraismes: journaliste pontoisienne : une féministe et libre-penseuse au xix*ᵉ siècle, actes du colloque Maria Deraismes, Pontoise, Karthala, 2001, Fabienne Leloup, *Maria Deraismes, riche, féministe et franc-maçonne*, Paris, éditions Michel de Maule, 2016.

178 Gisèle Hivert-Messeca, Yves Hivert-Messeca, Cécile Révauger, Femmes et franc-maçonnerie : trois siècles de franc-maçonnerie féminine et mixte en France (1740 à nos jours), Paris, Dervy, 2015.

179 Andrée Prat et Colette Loubatière, *L'ordre maçonnique, le Droit humain*, PUF, coll. ""Que sais-je"," 2003.

180 Alexandra David, "Le féminisme rationnel," *Editions de la Société nouvelle*, May 19, 1909. Re-edited in *Féministe et libertaire, Ecrits de jeunesse*, Paris, Éditions Les nuits rouges, 2013, pp.97-102.

181 Alexandra David, Féministe et libertaire, Ecrits de jeunesse, op.cit., pp.97-102.

182 Ibid., pp.98-99.

183 Ibid., p.99.

184 Ibid., p.99.

185 Ibid., p.100.

186 Lenard R. Berlanstein, *Daughters of Eve. A Cultural History of French Theater Women from the Old-Regime to the Fin-De-Siècle*, Harvard University Press, 2001.

187 Alexandra David-Néel, *Féministe et libertaire*, op.cit., p.130, "Question pressante."

188 Ibid., p.130.

189 "Le féminisme rationnel," Alexandra David-Néel , *Féministe et libertaire*, op.cit., p.194. Originally published in 1909.

190 Ibid., pp.132-133.

191 "Le féminisme rationnel," Ibid., p.194

192 Ibid., p.132.

193 Ibid., p.132.

194 Ibid., p.132.

195 Ibid., p.194.

196 "Le féminisme rationnel," op.cit., p.188. She mentions Charles Letourneau, *L'Évolution du mariage et de la famille*, and writes that his work enables us to scientifically understand the 'different phases of women's servitude in history'. The

meaning she gives to 'science' here is the collection of data about marriage and family in different cultures and among animals and the relativist and naturalist conclusion that humans should behave as animals. Science, according to Letourneau and to her, shows that morality, religion, laws, customs, and other sociocultural facts are just fabricated conventions with no value whatsoever.

197   Ibid., p.219.

198   Ibid., p.138.

199   In England, the Theosophist Annie Besant, with whom Louise David corresponded, was one of the first women to advocate for planned parenthood. See Muriel Pécastaing-Boissière, *Annie Besant (1847-1933): la lutte et la quête*, Paris, Adyar, 2015.

200   As she describes in her novel *Le Grand Art* and in her short story "Devant la face d'Allah. Conte du désert," Bruxelles, *Le Soir*, 1909.

201   Unpublished correspondence with her husband, Archives of the David-Néel Museum.

202   *Correspondance avec son mari*, op.cit., 25 september 1906.

203   The profession she declared at the city hall whe she married Philippe Néel.

204   *Le philosophe Meh-ti (ou Mo-Tse) et l'idée de solidarité*, Londres, Luzac et Cie, 1907; *Les théories individualistes dans la philosophie chinoise*, Paris, Giard et Brière, 1909; *Le modernisme bouddhiste et le bouddhisme du Bouddha*, Paris, Alcan, 1911.

205   Alexandra David-Néel, *Correspondance avec son mari*, op.cit., 10 Aug. 1911, pp.84-85.

206   David-Néel first wrote and published on Mozi, then on Yang Zhu: in 1906 she published an article entitled "L'idée de solidarité en Chine au Ve siècle avant notre ère. Le philosophe Meh-ti," in *Bulletins et Mémoires de la Société d'anthropologie de Paris* 5 no. 7, pp.334-342, and then expanded the text into a book titled *Le philosophe Meh-ti et l'idée de solidarité*, coll. Socialisme chinois, London, Luzac et Co, 1907. The next year she published an article on Yang Zhu entitled "Un 'Stirner' chinois," *Mercure de France* 76, 1908, no. 275, pp.445-452, which became a book in 1909: *Les Théories individualistes dans la philosophie chinoise: Yang-Tchou*, Paris, Giard et Brière, 1909. The two books were re-edited posthumously and published together as *En Chine. L'amour universel et l'individualisme intégral. Les maîtres Mo-tsé et Yang Tchou*, Paris, Plon, 1970.

207   She had received a grant from the French Ministry of Instruction to conduct research in India, National Archives, file n°F17-17281.

208   Alexandra David-Néel , *L'Inde, hier, aujourd'hui, demain*, Paris, Plon, 1951 (re-ed. as *L'Inde où j'ai vécu*, Paris, Plon, 1969).

209   She described Vivekananda as "haughty, cocky, almost arrogant." Letter to her husband, January 13, 1911, Archives of the David-Néel Museum, cited in Joëlle Désiré-Marchand, op.cit., pp.118-119.

210 Unpublished letter to her husband, March 19, 1912, Archives of the David-Néel Museum.

211 Both books were edited in Paris by Plon.

212 Both books were edited in Paris, by the Theosophical publishing company Adyar, and were re-edited together by the Editions du Rocher in 1958. The book has not been re-edited since then.

213 Alexandra David-Néel, *L'Inde où j'ai vécu*, op.cit., p.31.

214 Unpublished letter to her husband, January 21, 1912, Archives of the David-Néel Museum.

215 *L'Inde où j'ai vécu*, op.cit., p.31.

216 Unpublished correspondence and notes, Archives of the David-Néel Museum.

217 *Correspondance avec son mari*, op.cit., p.93 and p.97. Charles Webster Leadbeater (1854-1934) was a former Anglican priest who became a Theosophist. He was close to Annie Besant, who readmitted him in the Society after he had been accused of pederasty (1906). He spent some time in India, supposedly to receive teachings from 'the Masters', and was instrumental in the discovery and training of Krishnamurti, the new messiah or 'World Teacher'. He later founded his own Theosophical Church, the Liberal Catholic Church. David-Néel apparently met him while he was in Adyar, and describes him in her posthumous book *Faits étranges et gens bizarres...*, op.cit.

218 Ibid., p.89.

219 Ibid., pp.90-91.

220 Ibid., pp.91-92.

221 Ibid., p.92.

222 Ibid., pp.92-93.

223 Alexandra David-Néel, *L'Inde où j'ai vécu*, p.185.

224 Aurobindo first published his thoughts in a monthly magazine he started in 1914, *Arya*, and later reworked his texts to publish them in book form. Some of the most famous are *Life Divine, The Synthesis of Yoga, The Ideal of Human Unity.*

225 Complete works by Mirra Alfassa and testimonies of disciples such as the French convert 'Satprem', *Mère*, Paris, Robert Laffont, 1977.

226 Alexandra David-Néel, *Correspondance avec son mari.*, op.cit., p.94.

227 Alexandra David-Néel, *L'Inde où j'ai vécu*, op.cit., p.236-237.

228 Alexandra David-Néel, *Correspondance avec son mari*, op.cit., p.95.

229 Ibid., op.cit., pp.123-124.

230 Alexandra David-Néel, *L'Inde où j'ai vécu*, op.cit., pp.236-250.

231 Alexandra David-Néel, *Correspondance avec son mari*, op.cit., p.108.

232 Ibid., p.110.

233   Ibid., pp.111-112.

234   Ibid., p.111-112.

235   Ibid., p.112. Shankaracharya, or Adi Shankara, was an 8th-century philosopher who wrote about Advaita Vedanta and is said to have unified the various philosophical doctrines of Hinduism.

236   Alexandra David-Néel, *Correspondance avec son mari*, p.121. She does not mention the titles of the texts she is translating.

237   Ibid., p.113.

238   Ibid., p.118.

239   Ibid., pp.113-114.

240   Ibid., pp.116-117.

241   Ibid., p.119.

242   Ibid., p.118.

243   Ibid., p.114.

244   Alexandra David-Néel, *L'Inde où j'ai vécu*, op.cit., pp.66-67.

245   Alexandra David-Néel, *Correspondance avec son mari*, p.124.

246   Romain Rolland, Gandhi, 1924, Vie de Ramakrishna, 1929, L'Inde vivante, 1929, Vie de Vivekananda, 1930.

247   Alexandra David-Néel, *Correspondance avec son mari*, p.103

248   Ibid., p.125.

249   Ibid., p.132.

250   Alexandra David-Néel, *L'Inde. Hier, aujourdhui, demain*, Paris, Plon, 1951, re-edited and augmented as *L'Inde où j'ai vécu*, Paris, Plon, 1969.

251   Alexandra David-Néel, *L'Inde où j'ai vécu*, op.cit., p.31.

252   Ibid., p.32-34.

253   To get rid of the *tulpa*, however, seems to be another story. The *tulpa* she created was a monk, she said, that was first a kind of obedient slave to her, but later he became a mischievous and noxious parasite that haunted her days and nights. Discussion with Marie-Madeleine Peyronnet (July 2017).

254   Ibid., p.178.

255   Ibid., p.238.

256   Ibid., p.247.

257   Ibid., pp.228-229.

258   Ibid., Chapter III, pp.42-56.

259   This is the title of her second chapter. Ibid., pp.31-41.

260 Ibid., pp.35-36.

261 Ibid., p.37.

262 Tibetan religious pratices had notably been documented by the British army officer and ethnographer Laurence Austine Waddell in *The Buddhism of Tibet: Or Lamaism, With Its Mystic Cults, Symbolism, and Mythology, and in Its Relation to Indian Buddhism*, 1895, which was well know to European orientalists, and earlier in *Relation de voyage* written by two Lazarist missionaries, Évariste Huc and Joseph Gabet, 1847.

263 Alexandra Myrial, "Le pouvoir religieux au Thibet. Ses origines," Paris, *Mercure de France*, V52, December 1904, pp.599-618.

264 Alexandra David-Néel, *Voyage d'une Parisienne à Lhassa*, Paris, Plon, 1927, reprinted in paperback, 1989, Introduction, p.6.

265 Alexandra Myrial, "Le pouvoir religieux au Thibet. Ses origines," op.cit., p.600.

266 Ibid., pp.602-603.

267 Alexandra David-Néel, *Correspondance avec son mari*, op.cit., Letter dated April 14, 1912, op.cit.pp.141-148.

268 Alexandra David-Néel, *Voyage d'une Parisienne à Lhassa* (1927), reprinted,1989, p.5-6.

269 Alexandra David-Néel, *Correspondance avec son mari*, op.cit., pp.144 (letter dated April 14 1912).

270 Ibid., p.146 (letter dated April 15, 1912).

271 Ibid., p.147 (letter dated April 15, 1912).

272 Ibid., pp.189-193 (letter dated June 25, 1912).

273 Alexandra David, "Auprès du Dalaï Lama," *Mercure de France*, n°367, Tome XCIX, 1er October 1912, pp.466-476.

274 Ibid., p.466.

275 Charles Bell, *Portrait of a Dalai Lama: The Life and Times of the Great Thirteenth*, London, Collins, 1946 (reprint, Wisdom Publication, 1987).

276 Ibid., p.117ff..

277 "Auprès du Dalaï-Lama," op.cit., pp.465-466.

278 Ibid, p.469.

279 Ibid., p.468.

280 Ibid., p.471.

281 Ibid., p.471.

282 Ibid., p.475.

283 *Correspondance avec son mari*, letter dated June 25, 1912, op.cit., p.191.

284 "Auprès du Dalaï Lama," op.cit., pp.469-470.

285 Ibid., p.470.

286 Cf. notably Anagarika Govinda (Ernst Lothar Hoffman), who mentions this holy man in

The Way of the White Clouds, 1966, French trad. Française : Le Chemin des nuages blancs. Pèlerinages d'un moine bouddhiste au Tibet.

287 *Correspondance avec son mari*, op.cit., letter dated May 28, 1912, pp.167-169.

288 *Correspondance avec son mari*, op.cit., letter dated May 28, 1912, pp.167-169.

289 Ibid., letter dated May 30, 1912, pp.173-175.

290 Ibid., lettre dated May 28, 1912, p.175.

291 Ibid., p.143 (letter dated April 14, 1912).

292 Ibid., letter dated May 28, 1912, p.172.

293 Quoted by Joëlle Désiré-Marchand, op.cit., p.138. I have unfortunately not been able to trace this document nor any kind of reform project in the Alexandra David-Néel archives.

294 *Correspondance avec son mari*, op.cit., pp.185-186 (letter dated June 23, 1912).

295 Donald Lopez, *The Tibetan Book of the Dead – A Biography*, Princeton University Press, 2011.

296 *Correspondance avec son mari*, op.cit., p.143 (letter dated April 14, 1912).

297 Alexandra David-Néel, *Mystiques et magiciens du Tibet*, Paris, Plon, 1929. Reprint, 1980.

298 Ibid., pp.24-28.

299 *Correspondance avec son mari*, op.cit., p.302 (letter dated March 18, 1914).

300 Ibid., letter dated March 18, 1914, p.303. The two ritual rings in question had been given to her by the gömen of Lachen some time earlier. They are on display at the Alexandra David-Néel museum, Digne-les-Bains.

301 Ibid., letter dated March 28, 1912, p.303.

302 Robert E. Buswell Jr, Donald S. Lopez Jr, "rdzogs chen (dzokchen)," *The Princeton Dictionary of Buddhism*, Princeton University Press, 2014, pp.707-708.

303 Alexandra David-Néel, letter dated October 27, 1914, Archives de la Maison Alexandra David-Néel .

304 Alexandra David-Néel, *Initiations lamaïques*, op.cit., p.129, note n°2, in which she mentions the higher-stage teachings (spiritual exercises?) of the doctrines *ati anuttara* yoga professed by the Dzogstechén sect. These she describes by following the Tibetan expression "blana med pa," meaning literally "That which is supérieur does not exist."

305 Alexandra David-Néel, *Initiations lamaïques*, Paris, Adyar, 1930, reprint, 1957, pp.128-149.

306 Ibid., pp.130-138.

307 Alexandra David-Néel, *Mystiques et magiciens du Tibet*, op.cit., pp.209-210.

308 Alexandra David-Néel, *Mystiques et magiciens du Tibet*, Paris, Plon, 1929, paperback edition,1980, pp.207-248.

309 Alexandra David-Néel, *Correspondance avec son mari*, op.cit., pp.411 (letter dated March 16, 1916) and following.

310 Alexandra David-Néel, *Mystiques et magiciens du Tibet*, op.cit., notably p.234.

311 Ibid., pp.235-236.

312 Ibid., p.236.

313 Cf. for example the research conducted by the *Mind and Life Institute*, which sets out to prove the effects on the brain of meditation associated with religious ritual.

314 Alexandra David-Néel, *Correspondance avec son mari*, op.cit., p.371 (May 16, 1915).

315 Ibid., p.414 (April 3, 1916).

316 Undated letter from Alexandra David-Néel to the Gomchen of Lachen, archives of the Alexandra David-Néel Museum.

317 Anagarika Govinda, *The Way of the White Clouds*, London, 1966.

318 This book was first published in English in New York in 1925 to ensure the widest possible circulation.

CPSIA information can be obtained
at www.ICGtesting.com
Printed in the USA
BVHW080318121121
621442BV00008B/321